INSIGHT PO
D0196832

VIETNAM

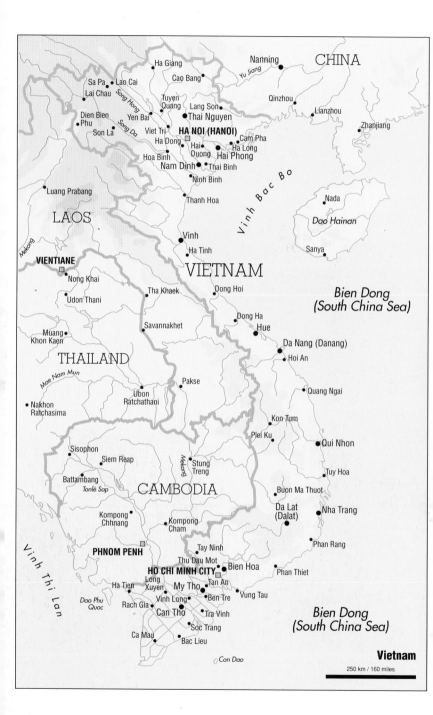

Vietnam

250 km / 160 miles

Welcome

T his guidebook combines the interests and enthusiasms of two of the world's best-known information providers: Insight Guides, who have set the standard for visual travel guides since 1970, and Discovery Channel, the world's premier source of non-fiction television programming. Its aim is to bring you the best of Vietnam in a series of tailor-made itineraries devised by Insight's Vietnam correspondent, Lucy Forwood.

Now is the time to visit Vietnam as she opens her doors to visitors from all over the world. This gracious land, long synonymous with conflict and revolution, has much to offer visitors: ancient Cham ruins, majestic pagodas, verdant landscapes, hideaway resorts and mind-blowing adventure trips. Then there are the people, who, despite undergoing a thousand years of Chinese rule, a century of French colonialism, and a troubled few decades of American influence, have remained indomitably Vietnamese in spirit and character. The carefully-planned itineraries in this book centre in and around the major hubs: Ho Chi Minh City and the south; the resorts of Dalat and Nha Trang; the Central Coast area; and Hanoi and the north. You could either choose to cover specific regions of Vietnam if pressed for time, or string the various itineraries together for an extensive tour of the entire country. Chapters on shopping, eating out and nightlife, plus a useful practical information section on travel essentials complete this reader-friendly guide.

Lucy Forwood has lived in Vietnam with her husband since 1992 and speaks animatedly of its people. 'If there's one spirit that you can't escape in this country,' says Forwood, 'it's the irrepressible optimism of the Vietnamese.' And it's so infectious, she guarantees that when you leave you'll bring something of that optimism home with you. Working as a freelance writer keeps her on top of the country as it metamorphoses and its war-torn past is laid to rest. Vietnam is not an easy country to discover on your own, as you'll soon learn. Forwood helps to minimize the runaround, and in the process uncovers for you the enigma that is Vietnam.

Pages 2/3: beach bikers at Nha Trang
Pages 8/9: boats at picturesque Halong Bay

History & Culture

'We have sometimes been weak and sometimes powerful, but at no time have we suffered from a lack of heroes,' declaimed Vietnamese scholar Nguyen Trai in the 15th century. Vietnam's history is one of heroic struggle against foreign menaces. Also, it is the history of several cultures. The differences that came to a head between North and South Vietnam in the 19th century stemmed in part from historic regional disparities and rivalries as well as cultural differences.

Early History

Legend has it that Vietnam emerged from a union between the King of the Sea, Lac Long Quan, and the Goddess Au Co. Half of their 100 sons lived with the father in the sea while the others lived with the mother in the mountains. From the latter group sprang the Au Lac nation and its people, the Lac Viet – the fusion point of legend and history. Au Lac developed a sophisticated culture by the 2nd century BC, prospering from Sino-Indian trade, and its remains still exist at Co Loa, its capital 16km (10 miles) north of Hanoi. Present-day Vietnamese recognise the Lac Viet as their forefathers, who left behind the legacy of the Dong Son drums. Made with technology advanced for the time, the drums have designs that depict dancing figures and musical instruments in concentric circles around a central sun-burst.

Between the 1st and 6th century, the Funan empire rose in the Mekong Delta. An Indian-based culture, Funan was known for its ornate art and innovative canal irrigation systems. Funan also depended on the thriving Sino-Indian trade and foundered when shipbuilding techniques improved and Oc Eo, the empire's main port near Rach Gia, was bypassed.

The era of the Hindu kingdom of Champa, from the 7th to the 14th century, was in many ways Vietnam's greatest. Champa was a federation of states, with the greatest of these, the kingdom of Amaravati near Danang. Each state had its own king, army, capital, religious site and port, and at one time, the federation stretched from Ha Tien near Cambodia in the south to Phan Thiet in Thuan Hai province. The Chams prospered by trading timber and medicines for salt and other goods from maritime traders. But, the Chams were better traders than soldiers, and in the 19th century Champa fell to the Vietnamese. Many Chams married Vietnamese and today, 75,000 of their direct descendants exist, mainly around Phan Rang in the south.

Champa architecture was influenced by Indian-Hindu and Buddhist contacts and its remains are the most outstanding in Vietnam. Early Cham (pre-11th century) sculpture and temple decorations exhibit an Indian gentleness and sensuality.

Left: ancient Cham tower near Cam Ranh
Right: Po Nagar detail

The Spectre of China and Self Rule

As Funan prospered in the south, the Chinese gained ground in the north, ruling the area between the Red River and Yunnan from the 2nd to 10th century. The Chinese settled and introduced Buddhism, Taoism and Confucianism along with dikes and metal ploughs. However, the Vietnamese did not willingly accept foreign tutelage. In AD43, when the Chinese executed a Vietnamese feudal lord, his wife and sister-in-law – the so-called Trung sisters – rallied local chieftains, expelled the governor and proclaimed themselves queens. When the Chinese counterattacked, the sisters plunged to their deaths in the Hat Giang River.

After the fall of China's Tang dynasty, King Ngo Quyen defeated the Chinese at the Battle of the Bach Dang River in 938. He established a semi-independent Vietnamese state and the beginning of 800 years of independence. A Confucian administrative system was introduced, Buddhism flourished, the mandarin code of ethics was imbibed and the country prospered.

However, border disputes between the Chinese, the Trans (1225–1400) and the Chams continued. In 1771, the Tay Son brothers from a wealthy merchant family revolted against the Trinh clan in the north and the Nguyen in the south. They routed the Chinese at Dong Da and led the country to a short-lived unity.

Nguyen Anh, one of the defeated Nguyens, sought assistance from French priest Pigneau de Behaine, who had set up a seminary on Phu Quoc island. In 1787, Prince Canh, Nguyen Anh's son, accompanied Behaine to Versailles where the latter persuaded Louis XVI to send 1,650 trained soldiers to Vietnam. The French king later rescinded the order, but 400 French deserters helped Nguyen Anh push back the Tay Sons. Proclaiming himself Emperor Gia Long and thus ushering in the Nguyen dynasty, Nguyen Anh unified the country and established his capital at Hue in Central Vietnam.

French Colonialism and the Birth of Communism

Gia Long recognised French interests as expansionist, and kept the growing wave of Catholicism at bay, but his successor, Minh Mang, was actively hostile towards Christianity. During the 1830s, several priests and Vietnamese Catholics were executed. By the mid-19th century, France was prepared to use force both to protect the priesthood and the interests of imperial expansion. In 1847, the French attacked Tourane (Danang).

In 1862, Emperor Tu Duc, who took the throne in 1848, ceded three provinces near Saigon as well as the Con Dao islands (Poulo Condore), and later the Mekong Delta, to the French. He was eventually forced into turn-

Above: a 1686 map of Indochina

ing the whole country into a French protectorate. The southern part of the country was renamed Cochinchina, the central as Annam and the northern provinces as Tonkin. The next few decades saw the steady expansion of French rule.

Forced labour, high taxes and a continuous French presence led to rebellions, which the French crushed mercilessly. Two emperors were exiled to Reunion in the Indian Ocean for planning revolutions and many Vietnamese were sent to the notorious Poulo Condore prison or the guillotine.

Several nationalist factions appeared, but none was more successful than the Communists. In 1911, Ho Chi Minh – the best known of many pseudonyms adopted by this charismatic leader – left for an 11-year sojourn in Europe, where he became a founder-member of the French Communist Party. At the Versailles Treaty following the end of World War I, he petitioned unsuccessfully for Vietnamese national self-determination.

After training in Moscow, Ho Chi Minh founded the Vietnamese Communist Party in Guangzhou (Canton). On his return to Vietnam in 1941, he formed the Viet Minh, a militant communist movement for independence.

The Consequences of World War II

Although France fell to Germany during World War II, an agreement with Japan enabled the French to continue its administration of Vietnam. However, towards the end of the war, the Japanese overthrew the French for fear of resistance. Vietnamese hatred for Japanese grew, especially when the latter's agricultural policies caused a severe famine in the north.

Following Japanese capitulation on 15 August 1945, Ho Chi Minh declared Vietnam a Democratic Republic. To safeguard colonial interests, the Potsdam Conference to clear up the aftermath of the war

Above: the 1847 French attack on Danang
Right: Viceroy of Tonkin

resolved that the Chinese Kuomintang soldiers accept the Japanese surrender north of the 16th Parallel while British forces assumed control in the south. British forces arrived in Saigon to find it in a state of anarchy. They released imprisoned French soldiers and even used Japanese troops to curb the Vietnamese. The response was a general strike. As the situation worsened, Emperor Bao Dai (1925–45) abdicated in favour of Ho Chi Minh. A year later, French boats shelled Haiphong after a 'customs dispute' and the First Indochina War broke out soon after.

Ho Chi Minh and the Viet Minh fled to the hills and waged a guerrilla war against the French that culminated in victory at Dien Bien Phu in 1954. At the Geneva Conference in July 1954, the French and Vietnamese agreed to partition the country into two states at the 17th Parallel. The northern half of Vietnam (Democratic Republic of Vietnam) was in Ho Chi Minh's hands and the southern half (Republic of South Vietnam) in those of the staunchly anti-communist Ngo Dinh Diem. Ho Chi Minh died in 1969 without seeing his dream of a united, independent Vietnam fulfilled.

The American Litany of Errors

Meanwhile, the US was interpreting the war in Vietnam as a sign that Indochina was the next front in the global war against Communism. By 1953, the US was bearing 80 percent of the French cost of the war in Vietnam.

In 1963, the US was further drawn into the Vietnam quagmire with the sending of over 16,000 military advisers to South Vietnam. The first American combat troops arrived in Danang in 1965, following the 'Tonkin Incident', in which a US warship, travelling illegally in North Vietnamese waters, was attacked by the North Vietnamese Army (NVA).

Thus began a catalogue of American misjudgments that ended only with

history/culture

the withdrawal of US combat troops in 1973 and the overthrow of the US-backed South Vietnamese regime in 1975. The American misadventure in Vietnam is sufficiently recent and so extensively documented (see *Further Reading*, page 99) that one need not dwell on it in detail. Suffice it to say that:

• The US-backed South Vietnamese President Ngo Dinh Diem was the worst possible man for consolidating anti-Communist support. A Catholic who hated other religions, Diem so provoked the Buddhists that in 1963, Venerable Thich Quang Duc committed self-immolation in public. Before the nepotic Diem and his brother Ngo Dinh Nhu were assassinated during a coup in 1963, many South Vietnamese had begun to see Diem as a puppet of the Americans and began to support the Viet Cong (VC), or Vietnamese Communists, the resistance fighters who succeeded the Viet Minh in the south.

• On 31 January 1968, as the Vietnamese celebrated the Lunar New Year (Tet), the Viet Cong launched an offensive in nearly 100 cities and towns, including Saigon, in what is known as the Tet Offensive, perhaps the most important series of battles during the American War in Vietnam. The Tet Offensive left Americans at home confused over the US's role in Vietnam. The Viet Cong's occupation of the US Embassy's compound in Saigon was seen on prime-time television by millions, and American public pressure mounted on President Lyndon Johnson to change his policies.

In 1973, the last American combat troops left Vietnam. On 30 April 1975, NVA forces arrived, victorious, in Saigon. South Vietnam's ARVN (Army of the Republic of Vietnam) had collapsed despite putting up bitter but isolated resistance.

Reunification

In July 1976, the Socialist Republic of Vietnam was founded. Reunified Vietnam was socialised, collectivised and sanitised. Close to 2 million people left Vietnam by land or by sea – the 'boat people' – to escape the new regime's economic policies and reprisals. The NVA was back in action in 1978, ending Pol Pot's reign of terror in Cambodia, but further offending China, which supported the Khmer Rouge. This and discrimination against Vietnam's influential ethnic Chinese community led to a brief invasion of the north by the Chinese in February 1979.

The xenophobic policies of the Vietnamese government forced the country into isolation and a close alliance with the former Soviet Union. Overseas trade was hindered by the US trade embargo, in place since 1975.

Rebirth of a Nation

In 1988, the concept of *doi moi*, or economic renovation, was introduced. Thus began the move towards a market economy. Privatisation began, small businesses proliferated and brave southerners dug up gold stashes and

Top Left: the Ho Chi Minh Mausoleum in Hanoi **Above:** faces of new Vietnam
Left: South Vietnam's ARVN forces in a reconnaissance mission

mobilised funds. However, despite increasing economic openness, the authorities still tread carefully in the area of social or political reforms.

Since the Asian economic crisis of 1997, Vietnam's economic liberalisation appears to have slowed, and the government has been criticised for its often haphazard reversal of economic policies. Although the US lifted the trade embargo in 1994 and cemented the relationship further in 2001 with a trade agreement, US-Vietnam economic ties are still fraught with difficulty. Foreign investors are making a tentative return today but are still wary of corruption in the government and regulations which are opaque. And while Vietnam is looking forward to long-term economic prosperity, it's not clear how this prosperity will be distributed among the people. The per capita income is slightly over US$500, and while Hanoi, Ho Chi Minh City and other major cities attract the most investments and enjoy rising incomes, the rest of the country is still an agricultural backwater with 75 percent of the population.

Ethnic Minorities

Ethnologists have classified 54 ethnic groups in Vietnam, with the Viet or ethnic Vietnamese making up 87 percent of the total population of 83.5 million people. The 1.7 million Chinese, or Hoa, who constitute the largest minority group, mostly live in the south and have become closely integrated with the Vietnamese. The other ethnic minorities, who make up the remaining 10 million, are hilltribes known as *nguoi dan toc*, or montagnards (mountain people) as the French called them. Most live on remote but spectacular mountains in the Northern or Central Highlands. Ethnically distinct from the montagnards are the Chams and Khmers, who number around 1.3 million.

The earliest montagnards arrived 5,000 years ago, trekking from China and India, or sailing from Indonesia and the Pacific. Their beliefs revolve around animism, although some tribesmen, particularly those in the Central Highlands, are Christians. Most hold fast to their culture and traditions, especially rituals concerning birth and burial. Montagnards tend to be small scale farmers but a few groups practise shifting cultivation.

In the Northern Highlands, travellers can most easily meet ethnic minorities such as the Hmong (or Meo), the Tai, the Red Zao and the Nung. They are very hospitable and will happily offer you an evening meal as well as a place to spend the night. In the Central Highlands, the Bahnar, Jarai and Ede are more assimilated to the Vietnamese lifestyle, and are therefore less easy to stay with unofficially. Buon Me Thuot has a museum devoted to hilltribes, and nearby Ban Don is a good place to see elephants.

If you intend to spend time with any particular group you should find a translator, or at least buy a copy of the book, *Ethnic Minorities in Vietnam*, published by The Gioi Publishers, Hanoi.

Left: hilltribe lasses at Sa Pa

HISTORY HIGHLIGHTS

258 BC Thuc Pan establishes a new Vietnamese state called Au Lac.

207 BC Trieu Da, a renegade Chinese general, conquers Au Lac and establishes power over Nam Viet in south China and northern Vietnam.

111 BC Chinese dominion over Vietnam is confirmed when the heirs of Trieu Da submit to the Han emperor.

AD 40 The Trung sisters lead the first major rebellion against the Chinese.

938 Ngo Quyen wins battle at Bach Dang, ending a millennium of Chinese rule.

1516 Portuguese seafarers are first Westerners to arrive in Vietnam.

1539–1778 Trinh Lords dominate the north while Nguyen Lords take control of the south.

1802–19 Nguyen Anh defeats Tay Sons and proclaims himself Emperor Gia Long, establishing the Nguyen dynasty.

1820–40 Emperor Minh Mang hostile to Christianity during his reign.

1861 French forces capture Saigon.

1862 Tu Duc signs a compromising peace treaty with the French.

1883 France establishes protectorate over Annam and Tonkin, and rules Cochinchina as a colony.

1890 Birth of Ho Chi Minh.

1930 Ho forms the Vietnamese Communist Party.

1940 Japan occupies Vietnam, leaving French administration intact.

1945 Japan defeated; Ho Chi Minh declares independence and Vietnam a Democratic Republic.

1946 French bombard Haiphong. Viet Minh withdraws from Hanoi. First Indochina War begins.

1954 Battle of Dien Bien Phu. Geneva Accord divides Vietnam. South Vietnam is led by authoritarian Catholic Ngo Dinh Diem, and North Vietnam by Communist Ho Chi Minh.

1955 Diem refuses to hold general elections. Land reforms in North Vietnam. Second Indochina War begins.

1960 North Vietnam introduces conscription. First US advisers in South.

1965 US President Johnson commences bombing of North; first US combat troops land at Danang in South.

1968 US troops rises to 540,000, but Tet Offensive saps morale.

1969 Ho Chi Minh dies aged 79; US begins phased withdrawal of troops.

1973 Washington and Hanoi sign cease-fire. Last US troops withdrawn.

1975 NVA captures Saigon. Vietnam reunified. US imposes trade embargo.

1976 Socialist Republic of Vietnam is declared. Communist regime in Cambodia begins territorial aggression.

1978 Cambodian troops mount cross-border attacks into southern Vietnam. Vietnam responds by invading Cambodia. Pol Pot government is overthrown.

1979 China retaliates by short invasion of northern Vietnam.

1986 6th Party Congress embraces *doi moi* (economic renovation).

1991 China relations normalised.

1993 Restrictions on Vietnam borrowing from IMF are lifted.

1994 US Trade Embargo lifted. Foreign investment tops US$10 billion.

1995 Vietnam becomes an official member of ASEAN (Association of Southeast Asian Nations).

1997 Economic reforms stall and foreign investors take flight.

2000 Bill Clinton becomes the first US President to visit since the war.

2001 The US and Vietnam sign a trade agreement.

2003 Vietnam hosts 22nd SEA Games.

2004 Foreign investors make a tentative return to Vietnam.

2005 Preparations for WTO acceptance include legal reforms and crackdowns on corruption.

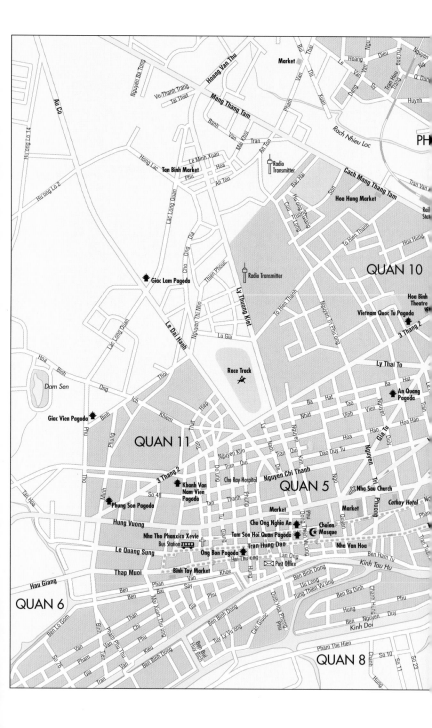

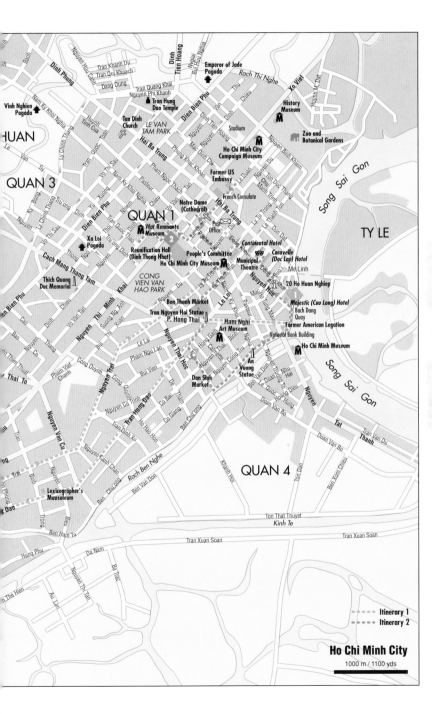

Ho Chi Minh City

1000 m / 1100 yds

— — — Itinerary 1
— — — Itinerary 2

Ho Chi Minh City
& the South

On 30 April 1975, the camera that had focused on South Vietnam for decades was abruptly blanked out. The final images seen in the West were those of the fall of the South Vietnamese capital Saigon: the roof of the US Embassy where the last departing helicopter was battling with crowds scrambling for space, desperate, terror-ridden faces, and tanks storming through the gates of the Presidential Palace.

While the much-feared massacre failed to materialise, what followed were 15 long years of deprivation and austerity as the victorious Northerners imposed their strict Stalinist interpretation of land reform and restrictions on free trade on the Southerners. It was a period of misery and discontent which caused hundreds of thousands to flee their homeland for other parts of Asia by sea in small boats. Many of such 'boat people' died of starvation at sea or when the boats capsized, while others were sent to malarial so-called 'New Economic Zones' in remote parts of Vietnam for 're-education'.

Since the 1990s, however, Ho Chi Minh City has risen, phoenix-like, from the ashes of former Saigon. The sprawling mass of humanity that is Vietnam's commercial capital today is still essentially defined by its previous incarnations. The graceful curves of French colonial buildings, 1960s contortions in ferro-concrete, Soviet-inspired 'bunker' architecture and currently neo-classical wedding cake all jostle for space along the boulevards and alleys that form the city. The residue of foreign influences remains as a pantheon of architecture.

Lying at the base of an S-shaped Vietnam, Ho Chi Minh City is bordered by the Saigon River to the east and a flat plain stretching as far as Phnom Penh in Cambodia, 245km (152 miles) to the west. Some 100km (62 miles) southwest, the Mekong Delta widens to greet the pounding waves of the South China Sea. The unwieldy megalopolis that now bears the name of the father of Vietnam's independence embraces Saigon and its twin, the predominantly ethnic Chinese city of Cholon, as well as great tracts of farmland.

Over 6 million people call this city home, and the number seems set to increase. The amiable Saigonese is blessed with a keen commercial eye and a heartwarming smile. You will not find a friendlier city. After decades of repression, Ho Chi Minh City has now set its course firmly in Vietnam's fast lane, making Hanoi seem staid and slow by comparison. Hotels have sprouted furiously, new bars and nightclubs open on a regular basis, and the traffic seems to double every dry season. Clamber onto a *cyclo* (trishaw) and throw yourself into the mêlée.

Left: a *cyclo* driver in Ho Chi Minh City
Right: statue of Ho Chi Minh

1. THE QUIET AMERICAN TOUR *(see map, p18–9)*

Day tour inspired by Graham Greene's novel, *The Quiet American*, visiting Ho Chi Minh City's main shopping streets and Cholon (literally Big Market, or Chinatown). Breakfast on top of the Majestic Hotel overlooking the Saigon River and stroll down Dong Khoi Street to browse at its boutiques. Cyclo to Cholon, the setting for gambling dens and anti-government agitators in 1954.

It is a good idea to read *The Quiet American* before setting out. In the novel, Graham Greene's Fowler attempts to lay bare the bones of one of Saigon's most Machiavellian eras. Set in the twilight of French influence, the novel recalls a murky 'what might have been' scenario tracing the outset of US involvement in Vietnam. Greene's Saigon is filled with war correspondents, doomed innocents and glasses of vermouth cassis.

Take a *cyclo* or walk to the prestigious **Majestic Hotel** at 1 Dong Khoi Street. Originally built in 1925, this old classic has undergone numerous renovations, the last in 1995. The roof commands one of the best views of **Saigon River** but even if you don't feel like a rooftop breakfast, do go up there to have a look. To your left lies the old Saigon port and to your right the new one. The impressive salmon-pink building to your right is the old customs house, nicknamed Dragon House, built by a French mercantile company in 1862. This is where Ho Chi Minh, who formed the Vietnamese communist movement in the 1930s, set off as a galley boy to discover Europe and Communism. The building is now the **Ho Chi Minh Museum** (open daily 8–11.30am and 2–6pm, closed Mon and Fri afternoons; admission fee) and displays photographs of this great leader together with many of his personal artefacts such as clothing, sandals, radio and other memorabilia. Ahead of you lies the Thu Thiem district. Plans are afoot to turn this area into an industrial zone, so enjoy the expansive views of the city while you can.

Main Shopping Streets

Turn left out of the main entrance of the Majestic and as you walk up **Dong Khoi Street** away from the river, cast your imagination back to the early 1900s, when the street was known as Rue Catinat. During French colonial days, Rue Catinat was an elegant street, lined with fashionable boutiques,

cafés and theatres. Later, it was renamed Tu Do by the Vietnamese and degenerated into a sleazy street lined with loud bars, fast women and other nocturnal temptations.

Today, Dong Khoi Street has regained its earlier prestige. Treat this expedition as a window-shopping spree: you can always go back and bargain for better prices. Dong Khoi offers a hotchpotch of items: amber, Russian watches, old fountain pens, cinnamon wood boxes, lacquerware and designer shops. Greene's opium dens no longer exist, but you can still buy a souvenir pipe. Don't be tempted by antiques. You cannot export them, and people are nearly always stopped, fined and have such goods confiscated.

Immediately to your left at No 21 is **Vietsilk** (tel: 08-823 4860), packed with an outstanding selection of silk clothing, pith helmets and silk jumpers. There are a number of fabric stores along Dong Khoi Street which sell both off-the-peg clothing as well as made-to-measure apparel in silk, cotton and linen. If you opt for the latter, give yourself two or three days to get measured, the outfit tailored and any necessary last minute adjustments made before you leave. (**Song** at No. 41 and **Khaisilk** at No. 107 further down Dong Khoi Street are particularly good stops; the latter also sells home assessories like silk cushion covers and tablecloths.)

At No 20 Ho Huan Nghiep Street to the right is the **Tiem Sach Bookstore**. The owner, who died in 1994, spent sleepless weeks ferrying heaps of books back and forth in the aftermath of Saigon's fall in 1975, saving them from a fate as bonfire fuel. The store has a good collection of mostly used French and English titles.

Old World Buildings

Cutting across Dong Khoi is **Mac Thi Buoi Street**, previously the Rue d'Ormay. This street housed one of the notorious opium dens that the protagonist Fowler was so fond of. In keeping with the city's current clean image it now has two of the best linen shops in the city, **Mai Anh** (tel: 08-829 5367) at No 81 and **Minh Huong** (tel: 08-822 3074) at No 85.

Lam Son Square which greets you was formerly the Place Garnier, the scene of General Thé's terrorist bombing in *The Quiet American*. Walk to the **Continental Hotel** on the northern side of the square, between Dong Khoi Street and Le Loi Boulevard. The hotel no longer has its famous Continental Shelf Café where Fowler used to sip on a vermouth cassis, but it does have a charming courtyard which serves a decent capuccino. Posters outside the **Municipal Theatre** between the **Caravelle Hotel** (where American hacks used to down brandies and sodas) and the Continental will tell you if there

Left: views of Saigon River from the Majestic Hotel
Above: express delivery in Ho Chi Minh City

is a performance, which could range from classical ballet and traditional theatre performances, to pop concerts and fashion shows. On weekends, around
the fountain, **Le Loi Street** brims with young Saigonese promenading in their
hippiest clothes.

Continue up Dong Khoi Street to 'the hideous pink Cathedral', Greene's
description of the **Notre Dame Cathedral** in the aftermath of the bombing
at Place Garnier. Services are conducted at 5am and 5pm but you can pop
inside at other times during the day to visit (recommended hours are Mon–Fri
8–10.30am, 3–4pm). The colonial-era **General Post Office** to the right is
open till 10pm. Head back to Lam Son Square and make a quick detour
right to see the **statue of Ho Chi Minh** in front of the fine old gingerbread
Town Hall, now the **People's Committee** building.

If you're tired of walking, negotiate with a *cyclo* for an hourly rate. Turn
into **Nguyen Hue Street** (Boulevard Charner), a bargain basement for SLR
cameras. Note the **Kho Bac Nha Nuoc** (Municipal Water Works) building

at 37 Nguyen Hue on your right as you head
towards the river. Turn up the next street, Ham
Nghi (formerly Boulevard de la Somme) and
glance at the **former American Legation** at 39
Ham Nghi street and **Ho Tung Mau Street**.
This unattractive 1950s block was where the
character Pyle conducted his nefarious affairs
a stone's throw from Mr Muoi's bomb factory.
Today, this street has the best bakery in town.
Nhu Lan at No 66 makes mouthwatering crois-
sants, breads and pastries. At 5.30pm you can
hardly get near the shop as workers descend
on it in droves.

Turn into **Tran Hung Dao Street**, the main
thoroughfare to Cholon in front of Ben Thanh
market. Here, fashion boutiques have opened
next to jeep showrooms. On some early morn-
ings, young daredevils turn the widest boulevard in town into an illicit motorcycle racetrack.

Cholon – the Chinatown District

Stop for lunch at one of the many restaurants dotted along this lengthy street
and then continue by *cyclo* towards **Cholon** – the Chinatown district, where
you'll see a curious building at **No 520**. This is the mausoleum to brilliant
scholar and lexicographer Petrus Truong Vinh Ky, who translated dictionaries
from Vietnamese into Cambodian and French. He is chiefly known for *Minh
Tam Buu Giam*, a Vietnamese version of Emily Post's book on etiquette. If
you can get into the little house inside the courtyard to the right you will
see where he lived, and a portrait of a 1930s Franco-Vietnamese family.

The approach to Cholon is marked by a furore of wedding dress shops –
bright, almost garish colours seem to be the latest trend – at the corner of
Tran Phu Street. Just before Tran Hung Dao Street becomes 'one-way', you
will see a gate on your left marked **Nha Van Hoa**, a venue for cultural activ-

Above: the Madonna welcomes visitors to the Notre Dame Cathedral

ities. This was previously the infamous Grande Monde Casino run by Bay Vien, the most notorious Chinese mafia leader of the 1950s.

Marking the end of Tran Hung Dao Street is **Nha Tho Phanxico Xevie** (St Francis Xavier Church), to which the hated President Ngo Dinh Diem and his brother Ngo Dinh Nhu fled during the palace coup in 1963. On the final approach to the church you will find the largest fabric market in town. You can buy cheap fabric here by the metre.

Make a right out of the church, go down the main road and turn right, and then second left to **Binh Tay Market** (open daily, 7.30am–6pm). To the left of the main gates is a sumptuous array of fruits and vegetables. Herbs such as cinnamon bark and star anise, and strange forms of noodles, dried mushrooms and other produce might keep you guessing their use for hours. If you venture further after the market to some alleys on your left you will find the area previously known as **Quai My Tho**, where Greene's antihero made contact with Communist insurgents. On your return, visit **Chu Ong Nghia An** at No 678 Nguyen Trai Street, a typical Chinese pagoda. A beautiful carved gold-painted wooden boat hangs over the entrance, and the interesting large spirals on the ceiling inside are incense coils which burn up to a week.

Finish the day with a vermouth cassis (Fowler's favourite tipple) at the **Q Bar** in the basement of the Municipal Theatre. Then go for a culinary adventure into authentic Vietnamese street food at **Quan An Ngon** (tel: 08-829 9449) at 138 Nam Ky Khoi Nghia. The owner literally ate his way around the streets of Ho Chi Minh City, seeking out the best 20 street stalls he could find before offering each of these cooks a job. The result – inexpensive mouthwatering street food in a very stylish setting.

Above: Nghia An Hoi Quan Pagoda
Right: a carved tiger in Chinatown

ho chi minh city & the south

2. THE WAR EXPERIENCE *(see map, p18–9)*

Morning tour of sights central to the fall of Vietnam in 1975, seeing the Reunification Hall, the War Remnants Museum and the site of the former US Embassy. After lunch, shop for US War memorabilia at Dan Sinh market. An evening drink at the Caravelle Hotel's Saigon Saigon Bar, followed by dinner at Tan Nam Restaurant.

Take a *cyclo* to the Dinh Thong Nhat or the **Reunification Hall** (open daily, 7.30–11am and 1–4pm; admission fee) at the corner of Nam Ky Khoi Nghia Street and Le Duan Boulevard. There's no more faithful expression of a megalomaniac's dream house than this piece of ostentation, which was formerly known as the Presidential Palace. Work on the edifice started shortly before President Diem's assassination in 1963, and by then, his helicopter pad, dance floor and cinema had already been planned. The architect, Ngo Viet Thu, a 1960s purist, designed details from chandeliers to carpets specifically for the palace, making it one of the few totally contemporary state buildings of this era.

As you enter the palace, linger over the poster-size photographs of the 1970s. One of these is the now famous image taken by NBC's Neil Davies of a Russian tank forcing down the palace gates on 30 April 1975, spelling the demise of South Vietnam and its government. General Duong Van Minh, South Vietnam's President for just 24 hours, surrendered to the northern forces minutes later.

Your guided tour around the Reunification Hall ends on the third floor with a succinct videotape lesson on Vietnamese history, spanning the defeat of the French colonial masters at Dien Bien Phu in 1954 to the overthrow of the US-backed South Vietnamese regime in April 1975, a worthwhile option if you can put up with the extremely poor soundtrack. Afterwards, you are free to

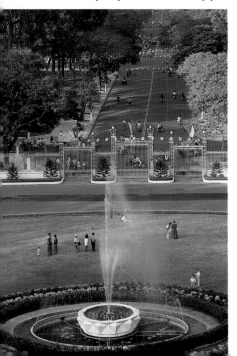

walk around the basement to see Nguyen Van Thieu's (president, 1967–75) war operations rooms, where there are some excellent maps of old Saigon.

Walk north (against the traffic) up Nam Ky Khoi Nghia Street to Vo Van Tan Street and turn left to find No 28, your next stop. The **War Remnants Museum** (open daily 7.30am–noon and 1.30–5pm; admission fee) resides in what was the headquarters of the US Information Services.

You need a strong stomach as the museum comes to grips with the nastier aspects of Vietnam's recent history, such as human embryos in jars and pictures of deformed children, depicting the effectiveness of the defoliant Agent Orange; gory photographs of war mutilations are also on display.

Left: Reunification Hall grounds

Although a visit here is likely to be distressing, it is a sobering reminder of the heavy toll of war and is a must-see for many visitors.

A new display, poignantly entitled **Requiem**, includes the art of photographers from many countries who died in various conflicts in Indochina. Outside in the forecourt, there is an impressive array of military hardware, and these include tanks, a helicopter, a fighter jet, and a guillotine used for decapitating agitators in the riots of the 1920s.

Backtrack towards the Reunification Hall. The gardens bordering Le Duan Boulevard were once the palace gardens. Walking towards the zoo, you'll see the **French Consulate** on your left, the only Western delegation to remain open throughout 1975 and afterwards. Take a peek through the rear entrance as the building is closed to the public.

At the crossroads with Mac Dinh Chi Street is the **US Embassy**, built over the original embassy building that was completed in 1967 (one of several diplomatic buildings designed by Edward Durrell Stone). The year following that, millions of television viewers watched agape as a Viet Cong special force broke into the embassy grounds during the Tet Offensive in 1968. The original building had another, greater, starring role when the last US helicopter left from its grounds in 1975, carrying a man aloft on a rope just seconds after the US Ambassador swept his country's flag away in ignominy and stepped into the helicopter. The building today houses the new US Consulate, signifying a new era in US-Vietnamese relations. Across the road, the tasteless blue-and-yellow structure was formerly the old British Embassy, which is now the British Consulate.

For lunch, walk down Pasteur Street to Nguyen Du, where at No. 80 **Nha Hang Com Ngon** serves traditional Vietnamese food in a stylish setting. Alternatively, **Dac Biet** offers 'special' *pho* at No. 75. This is a sidewalk eatery that is always busy, even if less salubrious than the former.

More War History

After lunch, take a *cyclo* to **Dan Sinh market** on Yersin and Nguyen Cong Tru streets. Among the hammocks and battery testing kits you'll find boots, parachutes and GI helmets. Not every item being sold here is original and you'll have to bargain.

Depending on the time, you could take a *cyclo* to the Bach Dang Quay for a boat trip. Take a leisurely ride along the canal – the possibility of doing this depends on the season and water level – to Cholon, or head for **Binh Quoi Tourist Village** (tel: 08-888 3018), some 8km (5 miles) north where you can have a Vietnamese dinner by the riverside while you are

Above: War Remnants Museum
Right: spiffy waiters at Tan Nam restaurant

ho chi minh city & the south

being serenaded by live traditional music. Friday is recommended for the hilltribe-inspired music. This place may be a tourist trap but its dinner is good value for money.

Alternatively, hop on a *cyclo* to the **Caravelle Hotel**, located at 19–23 Lam Son Square and have a drink at its **Saigon Saigon Bar**, which has one of the best views of the city and the river from its vantage point. The Caravelle was the place where American journalists holed up at during the war, and, despite a multi-million dollar refurbishment, it is still full of atmosphere. There are good restaurants at this hotel but I suggest that you walk along Dong Khoi Street to **Tan Nam** (tel: 08-829 8634) at 60–62 Dong Du Street – for a thoroughly civilised dinner in French colonial surroundings. The food, though, is Vietnamese, and very good.

3. CAO DAI TEMPLE & CU CHI TUNNELS *(see map, p30)*
Full-day trip to Cao Dai Temple, 'a Walt Disney fantasia of the East' according to Graham Greene. Spend the afternoon at the Cu Chi tunnels, home to the Viet Cong during the 1960s.

Organise a car or motorcycle taxi *(see page 93)*, commonly referred to as a *xeom*, from Pham Ngu Lao Street the day before for this long day trip. The back seat of a motorcycle is the best position for sightseeing in Vietnam but

it takes nerves of steel and a reasonably tough posterior. It could take up to 2½ hours to get to Tay Ninh province for the midday service at Cao Dai Temple. It's a good idea to wear clothes that will not show up dirt and are suitable for church, and take a torch if you intend to broach the tunnels. Alternatively, book a day trip with **Sinh Café** (tel: 08-836 7338) or one of the travel agents recommended on page 100.

Breakfast early and leave Ho Chi Minh City by 8am. The 96-km (60-mile) journey along Route 22 to Tay Ninh can take longer than expected. On the way, look out for duck herders with their long sticks keeping lines of ducks in order. The countryside is packed with lush ricefields, where water buffalo lounge and women are bent double sowing or harvesting rice.

As you near Tay Ninh, you will see **Nui Ba Den**, Black Lady Mountain. Towering 900m (2,953ft), the mountain pierces the skyline between Cambodia and Vietnam. The province borders Cambodia and many of the people here are Khmer, with a small Cham minority. The name of the mountain centres around the story of a principled lady who chose death to dishonour (a common Vietnamese tale). The Khmers regard the mountain as holy and there is a shrine near the top that you can climb up to in about 1½ hours. For the less athletically inclined, an effortless cable car ride takes the same route.

Above: pair of Cao Dai Temple worshippers

A Strange Church

On your way to **Cao Dai Temple**, reflect on its amazing history. During the 1920s, Ngo Van Chieu formed the Cao Dai religion, following a revelation of 'The Way' in a vivid dream. In 1926, one of his followers, Le Van Trung, deserted with 20,000 loyal disciples, crowned himself Pontiff and built the Cao Dai Temple at Tay Ninh. Seven years later, he was deposed for embezzling the temple funds.

By 1939, there were over 4 million Cao Dais, and by the mid-1950s, one in eight South Vietnamese was a Cao Dai. After World War II, both the Cao Dais and the Hoa Hao group (a breakaway Buddhist sect) dabbled in politics and formed private armies. Both sects had been useful in the fight against communism, but in the 1950s, many of the followers shifted their support to the Viet Cong. President Ngo Dinh Diem outlawed both sects in 1955, just after *The Quiet American* was written, for taking power into their own hands.

Cao Daism seeks to create the ultimate religion by fusing Buddhist, Taoist, Confucian and Catholic beliefs into a synthesis of its own. Today, 2 million Vietnamese still follow the Cao Dai way, but, sermons by planchette – originally, seances were held to contact 'saints' like Sun Yat Sen and Victor Hugo – are no longer practised. The authorities will not allow a new pontiff, knowing what skulduggery past leaders involved themselves in.

Still, tourists flock to the rather bizarre, brightly-coloured cathedral in droves, and the 'joke gone too far' (according to Greene) seems set to remain.

The Cao Dai Temple has eight stages in a progression leading to an altar and a huge orb-like eye. Each stage represents a step to heaven. Robed supplicants throng here for the 45-minute services during which you will hear traditional music being played. Services are held at 6am, midday, 6pm and midnight; most tours schedule their trips around the midday session.

Above: Cao Dai service in progress
Right: whipping up *trang bang*

ho chi minh city & *the south*

Life in the Tunnels

After the service (try to leave at 12.45pm), hurry back on the road towards Ho Chi Minh City: the **Cu Chi** tunnels (open daily, 7.30am–4pm; admission fee) are a 50-minute drive away. For lunch, head for **Trang Bang**, 400m (¼ mile) off the main road. **Nam Dung Restaurant** serves two specialities, *banh canh* and *trang bang*. The former is noodles with pork and bean sprouts and the latter, a do-it-yourself feast of pork, salad leaves, corn and herbs, wrapped in rice paper.

As early as 1948, the Viet Cong had begun to dig a huge network of tunnels in the heart of South Vietnam. The tunnels sheltered troops, held schools, hospitals, kitchens and stores, even multi-storied quarters. The lecture and displays will show ingenious U-bend openings leading to tunnels under rivers, and tiny openings where the Viet Cong stoically lived, fought and died.

Some tunnels at Cu Chi have been enlarged for foreigners to get a feel of how the Viet Cong lived. There is some doubt as to the tunnels' authenticity because of the heavy bombing in the area, but in any case you'll get the point that tunnel life – some women gave birth down there – was highly distasteful and only for the very brave. Cu Chi subsequently became the most densely bombed area in Vietnam and suffered heavy defoliation during the 1960s when the Americans, fed up with being ambushed, set about bombing the area out of existence.

Take a guided tour of the tunnels, built on three levels, for that wartime feel, and then return to Ho Chi Minh City.

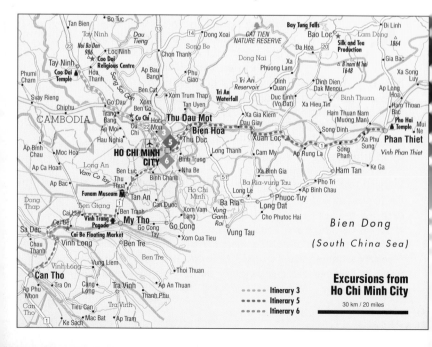

Excursions from Ho Chi Minh City

---- Itinerary 3
━━━━ Itinerary 5
▪▪▪▪ Itinerary 6

30 km / 20 miles

4. PHU QUOC *(see map, p32)*

A weekend away at Vietnam's paradise island. Breakfast by the beach, snorkel in pristine waters and look out for turtles and dugong, Odysseus's famous siren. After a seafood lunch on one of the many beaches, relax in a hammock or visit a fish sauce factory and pepper farm.

Vietnam's largest island, **Phu Quoc**, is located about 115km (77 miles) west of Rach Gia. This tear-shaped island is 50km (30 miles) long and covers some 1,300 sq km (500 sq miles). Located just 15km (11 miles) south of the coast of Cambodia, the mountainous and forested island has some of the

most beautiful beaches in Vietnam and a splendid abundance of marine life. The waters around the island are also sufficiently unpolluted for pearls to be cultivated in oyster beds.

The two main developed areas on the island are **Duong Dong**, where the airport is, and **An Thoi**, the main shipping port about 20km (12 miles) away, where the ferries arriving from Rach Gia and Ha Tien dock.

The island can be accessed by air from Ho Chi Minh City (4 times daily) as well as from Rach Gia (once daily). Visitors who prefer to travel overland can also take a morning speed boat service (about 8am) to the island from Rach Gia (2½ hours) or from Ha Tien (1½ hours). Rach Gia is 250km (155 miles) from Ho Chi Minh City, while Ha Tien is located 340km (210 miles) away.

French Foothold

In 1765, French seminarist Pigneau de Behaine was sent to Phu Quoc to train Roman Catholic missionaries. He was instrumental in helping Nguyen Anh, or Emperor Gia Long as he was later crowned, secure French military support against the Tay Son rebels, from whom Nguyen Anh was fleeing. In return for the French support, Nguyen Anh offered land. During the Vietnam war, Phu Quoc was used to hold Viet Cong prisoners. The main penal colony, known as **Coconut Prison** (open daily 7.30–11am and 1.30–5pm; free), is located near An Thoi town and still used as a prison.

Fish Sauce and Pepper

Phu Quoc is famous for its two traditional products: high-quality fish sauce (*nuoc mam*), which is exported globally, and black pepper. The former is so famous that throughout the years of the trade embargo, Thai fish sauce producers used a brand name, '*Phu quoc*', to market their own produce.

To harvest the anchovies for making the fish sauce, fishermen cast nets from boats not far offshore during the night and reel them in at sunrise. The whole fish are layered with sea salt and left in huge wooden barrels to fer-

Top left: Cu Chi tunnel network is a bit of a squeeze
Above: Long Beach, Phu Quoc island

ment between 6 months to a year, after which the resulting liquid is drawn off, filtered and then bottled. There may be subsequent extractions, but this first one is the highest in protein, the best flavoured and the most valued. If you would like to view the process, **Thanh Ha Fish Sauce Factory** (tel: 077-846 139; daily 7am–6pm; free) in Duong Dong welcomes tours (e-mail: thanhhaco@hcm.vnn.vn).

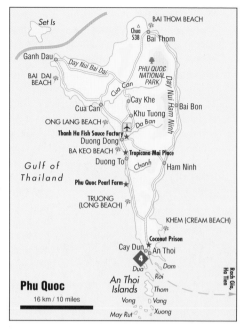

You may also wish to visit a pepper plantation. **Cassia Cottage** (tel: 077-848 395; e-mail: cassia cottage@cassiacottage. com), located at **Ba Keo** beach, 2km (1¼ miles) from the airport, can organise a visit. **Phu Quoc Pearl Farm** (tel: 088-980 585), 8km (5 miles) south of Duong Dong town, also has tours for visitors, and a retail shop from which pearls or pearl jewellery can be purchased.

Perfect Beaches

The miles of white sand beaches on Phu Quoc are its main draw. At the remote, northwestern side of the island are **Bai Dai** beach and **Ong Lang** beach. The most popular and most accessible is **Truong** (Long Beach), and this is also where most of the accommodation and restaurants are located. The beach stretches spectacularly from Duong Dong southward along the west coast and almost all the way to the port at An Thoi.

Khem (Cream Beach) on the southeastern side of the island, 2km (1¼ miles) from An Thoi, is the most beautiful. It is also totally undeveloped because it is a military area. Do check with your hotel before setting out, because visitors are sometimes not allowed to enter. To get there, you will need to hire a motorbike.

Phu Quoc National Park (open daily 7am–6pm; free) was established in 2001 in the hilly northeastern part of the island. **Chua Mountain**, the highest of the 99 peaks, is located within the park. Little, however, is as yet known about the biodiversity of the park's 37,000 ha (91,427 acres) of lowland evergreen forest, which covers almost a third of the island. Check with your hotel about obtaining a permit to visit the park, which is accessible by car as well as by motorbike taxi.

To the south of the island is the **An Thoi Archipelago**, a group of 15 islands popular with divers and snorkellers. The surrounding waters are home to the endangered dugong as well as the Leatherback and Hawksbill turtles, although underwater enthusiasts are more likely to see a large variety of small, colourful reef and coral fish, many of which are endemic to Vietnamese waters. To visit the outlying islands or to organise a dive trip, contact **Rainbow Divers** (tel: 058-524 351; www.divevietnam.com).

5. PHAN THIET *(see map, p30)*

The small fishing town of Phan Thiet is fast developing into one of Vietnam's most appealing coastal destinations because of its laid-back atmosphere and proximity to beautiful Mui Ne Beach

It's a 200-km (125-mile) 2½ hours drive from downtown Saigon to Phan Thiet on Route 1, the main highway to distant Hanoi. **Phan Thiet** is an attractive small fishing port, and there is a good range of accomodations on the beach to suit all budgets.

Phan Thiet was an outpost of the long lost kingdom of Champa; three small, rather undistinguished Cham Towers still stand about 5km (3 miles) east of the town to mark the fact. Today, the very few French villas that are still standing serve as a reminder of the colonial period. The French have gone but the descendents of the Chams, now much intermarried with the dominant Viets, still live here. The town lies at the mouth of the picturesque and busy Ca Ty River. The heart of the town lies to the west of the river, joined to the former colonial quarter to the east by Tran Hung Dao Bridge.

Until quite recently, with the advent of tourism, Phan Thiet was best known for producing some of the best *nuoc mam* or fish sauce in Vietnam, an important ingredient used in Vietnamese cuisine. Today, the fishing industry remains important, while speeding trucks loaded with fish sauce still represent a hazard near the port and on nearby Route 1. West of Tran Hung Dao the town fairly bustles with commerce, and the pungent smell of

Left: Duong Dong town on Phu Quoc island
Right: woman mending nets in Phan Thiet

nuoc mam hangs in the air. To the east of the bridge, some buildings belonging to the colonial period still retain some of their former glory, even as they sit among newer shops, hairdressing salons and *pho* stalls.

A Charming Town

It's best to explore the town by heading for the busy wharf-side area early in the morning – when markets are at their busiest. As fishing catches are also landed at this hour, the bustle is considerable. The atmosphere changes north of Tran Hung Dao Street. Here are the town's main temples, notably **Ong**

Pagoda, 161 Trang Hung Dao, where local women pray for children to the deity Me Sanh; and **Duc Thang**, perhaps the most attractive temple in town, somewhat dilapidated but covered with figures of celestial dragons and other creatures. This part of town also houses the large Central Market, the **Ho Chi Minh Museum** and – perhaps more unusually – **Duc Thanh School**, where the great man once worked, albeit briefly, as a teacher. There are a number of small restaurants scattered throughout this part of town, but the **Cay Bang Restaurant** at 2 Nguyen Dinh Chieu just outside the town is a favourite with visitors and Vietnamese alike.

However, few visitors come to Phan Thiet for the town's delights. The real appeal lies some 20km (12 miles) further east along the coast, where palm-fringed sand dunes meet the azure waters of the South China Sea. The road to Mui Ne Beach passes the 8th-century **Po Sha Na Cham Towers** at the Km 5 mark, then continues down the narrow Mui Ne Peninsula. Motorbikes and bicycles are readily available for hire both in Phan Thiet town, and at almost every hotel and guesthouse springing up along the way.

Beach Appeal

Mui Ne Beach is indeed lovely, stretching for about 12km (7.5 miles) of golden sand and clear water. The well-appointed **Victoria Phan Thiet** at Km 9 offers beautiful accommodation, fine views of the sea and the shifting sand dunes. Besides this, there are many more reasonable and perfectly adequate places on the road to Mui Ne, with more being developed each year.

Vietnamese visitors to Mui Ne generally come to marvel at its huge and undulating salmon-coloured sand dunes, and enjoy watching for hours as the wind from the sea sculpts the sand crests into different patterns. It's possible to walk inland through the dunes following the path of a tiny stream called **Suoi Tien** or 'Fairy Spring', though it's very easy to get sunburned in the sands, especially at midday when they are too hot to walk on without shoes.

Other activities available at Mui Ne include windsurfing, sailing, water-

Above: getting ready to set off to sea
Right: river life on Mekong Delta

skiing, snorkeling and fishing. It's possible to just sit in the shade and watch the distant Phan Thiet fishing fleet setting off to sea or returning to port. For now the sublime tranquillity of the scene remains unmarred by water scooters and jet skis. Along the beach and at nearby resorts there are numerous restaurants offering good food.

6. MEKONG DELTA *(see map, p30)*

This three-day trip to Vinh Long and Can Tho in the heart of the Mekong Delta lets you peek into the unhurried but productive lifestyles unique to this area. Meander through small waterways to floating markets and nearby islands, and relax in one of the area's munificent fruit orchards.

Hire a car or motorcycle from Pham Ngu Lao Street. Plan to leave Ho Chi Minh City in the afternoon for the 138-km (86-mile) 3-hour journey so that you arrive in Vinh Long in time to catch the sunset. Stay at the **Cuu Long Hotel** (tel: 070-823 656; fax: 070-823 848). Either go for one of the more expensive rooms overlooking the water (book a week in advance), or, for a more rustic atmosphere, book the garden house belonging to Cu Tao on Binh Hoa Phuoc island. For the latter, book with **Cuu Long Tourist** (tel: 070-823 616; fax: 070-823 357; e-mail: cuulongtourist@hcm.vnn.vn; www.cuulongtourist.net), in the Cuu Long Hotel. If extending the trip to Can Tho, book accommodations ahead as well.

The Mekong River flows over 4,500km (2,800 miles) from the frozen wastes of Tibet through China, Laos, Cambodia and finally Vietnam and into the sea. The nine provinces of the Delta area, beginning at Tan An, 40km (25 miles) from Ho Chi Minh City, are known as Cuu Long or Nine Dragons, in reference to the nine tributaries of the Mekong spilling into the South China Sea. The number 9 is considered lucky in Vietnamese geomancy, and the Mekong Delta has certainly been lucky for its inhabitants. Silt from the Himalayan plateau has made this area Vietnam's rice bowl. Unlike the Red River Delta in the north, there is little risk of flooding as the Tonle Sap Lake in Cambodia acts as a giant overflow for the Mekong.

Vinh Long, 34km (21 miles) from Can Tho, the region's economic centre and 70km (43 miles) from industrial My Tho, sprawls along the southern shore of the Tien Giang, or Upper Mekong River. The town is typical

of this region: small, friendly and without a bustling centre. There are a few architectural remnants from French colonial times, a market and a handful of hotels but, as with all this region, the main action is on and around the river.

The Mekong Delta has undergone a dramatic change in recent years. Since the government allowed farmers to lease land and start private businesses in 1983, the area has prospered beyond belief. Today, electric pumps irrigate paddy fields where women with buckets would have done so previously. Tractors chug along tarred roads and television aerials stand on leafy shack roofs, testimony to the area's development.

Watery Delights

After a 2½-hour drive from Ho Chi Minh City, you'll reach a suspension bridge just before Vinh Long. Previously the water was dotted with ferries, huge clanking workhorses that carry everything from the school bus to street vendors and weather-beaten farmers. Only Ben Tre province and a few minor roads are served by these lumbering machines today. The crossings are only a few minutes and will throw anyone enraptured by the film *The Lover* into a romantic reverie.

In Vinh Long, secure a boat, either for the next day or to take you to your guesthouse on Binh Hoa Phuoc island if you have booked a homestay. Boats from Cuu Long Tourist are fairly expensive, but its English-speaking guides are well informed and can explain some of the area's mysteries to you. Alternatively, go to the An Binh Boat Station and negotiate.

Settle back and enjoy the sunset over the Tien Giang River from the roof of Cuu Long Hotel or a nearby waterside café. The hotel restaurant is a thinly disguised brothel, and unless you eat with the girls, you will find it impossible to understand the menu. Go instead to **Phuong Thuy Restaurant**, located just beyond the hotel, which has an English menu and good *cha gio* (spring rolls). Or else, wander to the edge of the market and sample *hu*

tieu, a delicious local dish of noodles with pork.

Next morning, meet your boatman for the 3-hour ride to **Cai Be floating market** (open daily 7.30am–4.30pm). You'll have the afternoon to visit the fruit orchards in nearby An Binh and Binh Hoa Phuoc islands for an insight into Delta agriculture.

As you leave the dock, you will see all along the riverbank people at their household chores or washing (women often bathe with all their clothes on) and children playing in the water. Many families have small sampans. Look out for the ones with great eyes painted red and black on their prows: these are ocean-going vessels, painted so they can see their way safely to the sea. Depend-

Left: Cai Be floating market

ing on the season, you will see rice barges filled with bananas, mangosteens, Java apples or other tropical fruits. It is interesting to see how vegetables, flowers, fish and rice are traded from boats at the floating market. All along the shoreline, fish traps spear the water. Observe how elegantly the people conduct their lives, sitting erect and proud as they steer their boats with long-shafted propellers or nonchalantly row with their feet.

Head for **Nguyen Thanh Giao's (Ong Giao) house** in Binh Hoa Phuoc island, 'the manifestation of peace and embodiment of world friendliness' as one guest has described it in the visitor's book. The garden – filled with numerous bonsai trees – is an idyllic spot for a rest in a hammock with a book in hand, and it is even better for lunch. Elephant ear fish (*ca tai tuong*), the local speciality, is as large as a soup plate and delicately flavoured. Watch how the Vietnamese eat it wrapped in rice paper with salad, then dipped in a sauce.

Study your map for other gardens and orchards to visit (or ask the boatman to recommend some). This is where a guide will help if you are interested in finding out how the fruits are grown. Rambutans, longans – the most important fruit in this area – mangoes and pineapples all produce abundant crops in the Mekong Delta's rich alluvial soil.

Onward to Can Tho

About 45 minutes' drive and 34km (21 miles) southwest of Vinh Long is the major ferry centre of **Can Tho**, largest town and effective capital of the Mekong Delta. Here, where the presence of Vietnam's substantial Khmer Krom community begins to make itself felt – head out to **Munirangsyaram Pagoda** at 36 Hoa Binh Street to experience the atmosphere of a Therevada Buddhist temple very similar to those in Cambodia – minus the Bodhisattvas and Taoist spirits found in Vietnamese Mahayana temples. Can Tho is a good place to stay overnight, as the accommodation available is the best in the delta, and good restaurants are aplenty. Try **Vinh Loi** along the waterfront for excellent seafood and, if you're feeling brave, its snake wine as a nightcap.

It's a good idea to rise early and take a boat trip to see one of the local floating markets – but note that business slows down by 8.30am. There are two worthwhile floating markets near Can Tho: **Cai Rang** is about 5km (3 miles) southeast of the city centre, while **Phong Dien** lies about 20km (12 miles) to the southwest. If you're feeling energetic, Phong Dien is the better bet as it is far less crowded. Return to Can Tho for a leisurely lunch at the Ninh Kieu Hotel at 2 Hai Ba Trung and enjoy the riverside views. Don't stay too late, as it can take around 3 hours to drive back to Ho Chi Minh City.

Above: rural life on Mekong Delta

Da Lat &
Nha Trang

D a Lat and Nha Trang are magnetic hubs for domestic tourists from the
south, including honeymooners. It's easy to see why. The cool mountain climate of Da Lat (altitude: 4,921ft/1,500m), open spaces and
waterfalls is balm for those who need respite from the heat and sweat of
Ho Chi Minh City 300km (187 miles) away. Solitude and breathtaking scenery
await the traveller with just a little energy to roam around. Set by the banks
of the Cam Ly River, Da Lat was established on the orders of Paul Doumer,
then Governor of French Indochina, in the early 20th century. It proved
popular with the French, and also with the Vietnamese. One downside: too
often shabby Soviet-style buildings detract from attractive French colonial
architecture, and there is more than a little kitsch about the place.

Nha Trang, just 230km (143 miles) away down the spectacular Ngoan Muc
Pass, is the ultimate in relaxation and recreation, offering charming French
colonial hotels, an easy atmosphere, soft, white sands, coconut palms and
warm seas. The city is an attractive, medium-sized port of about 200,000 people with one of the best beaches in Vietnam. The waters are clear and clean,
and the offshore islands are ideal for snorkeling, scuba diving and fishing.

Then there is the added bonus of people-watching, specifically Vietnamese
at play. For whether they are driving *pedalo* swan boats in Da Lat's Valley
of Love and having their photographs taken dressed as Da Lat cowboys, or
splashing fully-clothed – nobody wants a suntan in this nation that sets a pre-
mium on fair skin – at the beaches of Nha Trang, the enjoyment of the Vietnamese on holiday is both spontaneous and infectious.

To get to Da Lat from Ho Chi Minh City, hire a car or take the 7.30am
bus from Sinh Café (tel: 08-836 7338). Or fly Vietnam Airlines – twice
daily, with a flying time of 45 minutes. From Da Lat, Nha Trang is some 5
hours away by road. Ask your hotel to organise a minibus for you, or hire
a car. All hotels organise sightseeing tours that finish in Nha Trang. If you
are travelling direct to Nha Trang from Ho Chi Minh City, there is a 12-
hour train ride, leaving at 5am and 5pm, but be aware that the journey is
both slow and uncomfortable. A
more popular alternative is by
minibus or taxi (6–8 hours). These
services can be arranged through
Sinh Café. If you prefer to fly, Vietnam Airlines operates thrice-daily
flights from Ho Chi Minh City direct
to Nha Trang.

If travelling from the north, Vietnam Air operates once-daily flights
from Hanoi, as well as nine flights
a week from Danang.

Left: Dalat tykes
Right: Nha Trang beach and harbour

7. DA LAT *(see map, p41)*

A picnic lunch by an Alpine waterfall, viewing orchids en route while keeping a lookout for hilltribes, and a visit to a serene pagoda. End the day with dinner in a French colonial villa.

Once in Da Lat, rent a car for the day. **Da Lat Tourist Travel Centre** at 1 Ngugen Thai Hoc (tel: 063-822 520; www.dalattourist.com) has well-kept vehicles. Hardened scramblers can hire a motorcycle from the cheaper hotels, but this is neither for first-time bikers, nor advisable during the rainy season (May to October). Be sure to check your brakes before you leave town. In the mid-rainy season you will need a four-wheel-drive vehicle. The road is reasonably steep in parts on your 2-hour journey to the Ankroet waterfalls, and signposts are promised for some time in the future.

But first, breakfast at the **Long Hoa Café**, Duong 3, Thang 2, for an experience in old world charm. Try Mrs Thai's homemade strawberry jam, fresh bread and hot chocolate, and order the best yoghurt in Vietnam from a nearby stall.

Then, make your way down the steps to the market and buy a picnic lunch. Buy salt and pepper separately from sandwich vendors if you don't want them to make you a sandwich, but you will never see a pair of chopsticks used more delicately. There is a wine shop at 2C Nguyen Van Troi Street, which sells reasonably good plonk. Bring your own corkscrew, or improvise.

Alpine Waterfalls and Tribes

Head for Ankroet past the Linh Son pagoda which you will visit on your return journey. As you leave the town heading northwest on Xo Viet Nghe Tinh Street towards Lat village and Lang Bian Mountain, look at the surrounding market gardens. Da Lat has some of Vietnam's freshest vegetables and fruits. Strawberries, mulberries, passionfruit and now asparagus and broccoli all wend their way from these slopes to dining tables from Ho Chi Minh City to Hanoi.

If it's springtime (December to February), be sure to visit the **orchid gardens** at the **Institute of Biology** (Phan Vien Sinh Hoc) on your left after about 4km (2½ miles). Over 200 varieties of exotic orchids thrive in Da Lat's nutrient-rich environment, and you'll see some of the prettiest flowers in Vietnam here. Formerly a seminary, the building now houses stuffed animals, sea creatures, birds and butterflies from the Dalat province.

Continue on the road to Lang Bian Mountain and turn left at the crossroads signposted Suoi Vang (Golden Stream) 17km (10½ miles). Turn right at the T-junction and fork right soon afterwards. It's all downhill from here. Keep right as you pass the hydro-electric power plant sign (Thuy Dien) and you will find yourself at the top of some waterfalls with a drop of about 15m (50ft).

Above: Dalat market scene

As your car trundles towards your destination, reflect on some of the names Da Lat has inspired locally over the decades. Renaming countries, towns and heroes is almost a national pastime in Vietnam, and more often verges towards overstatement than precision. Da Lat has so far achieved 'The City of Love', 'Le Petit Paris' and 'La Petite Geneve'. The **Ankroet Waterfalls** have several aliases: Suoi Vang, Golden Stream Lake and Dankia. While this region is dotted with hundreds of waterfalls and lakes, Ankroet's are the most easily explored, and some of the least visited. Just upstream, a hydro-electric power plant has been constructed, forming a wide lake perfect for picnicking beside if you prefer not to eat on the rocks. Don't venture too far up the road past the lake; it becomes increasingly rugged and there is no town for miles.

If you do not have time to travel to the north, take time to meet some ethnic minorities around Da Lat. Each tribe has its own unique lifestyle and traditions, and is fascinating to see first hand. Check with the tour companies to see if you need a permit for overnight stays in the villages. You can drink rice wine from jars – the taste ranges from something similar to

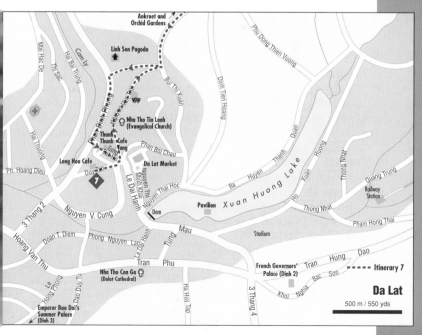

Above: cooling off at Ankroet waterfalls

an industrial by-product to a fair copy of *sake* – and listen to traditional music. If you're fortunate, you may well see some woodcutters or tribesmen walking in this area, carrying tall bunches of reeds to make into artefacts or weave into cloth. The minorities are generally shy people, and you must be quick when taking photographs.

About 12km (7 miles) northwest of Da Lat, at the base of Lang Bian Mountain, is a group of nine small settlements which make up **Lat Village**. This is an excellent place to go if you wish to see local hill peoples, still referred to by the French term Montagnards. Five of the settlements are inhabited by the Lat minority – hence the name of the place – whilst the other four settlements are inhabited by related minority groups, the Ma and the Chill.

On your return, stop off at **Linh Son Pagoda** on Phan Dinh Phung Street, fronted by two decorative dragon balustrades. If you arrive around 5pm, you will catch the monks chanting and beating their gongs. Look out for the screen in front of the altar with its unusual carved spiders. Built in 1938, the pagoda has a giant bell of bronze and gold.

If you need a warm cup of something, slip into **Café Tung** at 6 Khu Hoa Binh Street. Hot chocolate with rum is delicious as are the sticky cakes from **Pho Tung**, just a few doors up. For good Vietnamese food, dine at **Thanh Thanh** at 4 Tang Bat Ho Street. For French haute cuisine, the restaurant at Hotel Sofitel Da Lat Palace will not disappoint, but expect to pay dearly.

South of Da Lat

If staying in Da Lat longer than a day, make time to visit the thriving **central market** next morning, where apart from seeing an array of colourful fresh produce and handicrafts, you will encounter ethnic minorities, distinctive in their colourful dress. In the heart of town is **Xuan Huong Lake** where there are paddle boats and horse-drawn carts. The surrounding low hills, French-inspired villas and pine forests provide a lovely backdrop, although the water itself is muddy. South of the town is **Da Lat Cathedral**, built in 1931 and with stained glass windows from France. A few kilometres southwest is **Emperor Bao Dai's Summer Palace** or **Dinh 3** (open daily 7–11am, 1.30–4pm; admission fee) built in 1933 for Vietnam's last emperor. The 25-room villa displays pictures of Bao Dai and his family along with furniture used by the king.

Above: garden of Linh Son Pagoda
Right: outside Linh Son Pagoda

8. NHA TRANG *(see map, p44)*

Breakfast at the Bao Dai villas, then take a *cyclo* to Tran Phu Street to visit a museum dedicated to a brilliant medical researcher. Spend the rest of the day relaxing on the beach, or visit a Cham temple.

One of the loveliest spots in Nha Trang, rich with French colonial nostalgia, is the **Bao Dai Villas** (tel: 058-590 147; www.vngold.com.nt/baodai) beside Cau Da Port, originally built as royal accommodations for Bao Dai (1925–45), the last emperor of Vietnam. With large rooms painted in cool blues and lilacs looking out over the azure sea, these villas once housed the creme de la creme of Vietnamese society and high-ranking officials.

Breakfast at the villa is an experience you should not miss. Don't be in a hurry as the service does not allow for this. Instead, sit back and enjoy the garden setting, still the same as it was 70 years ago. Later, you might wish to see the emperor's bedroom, commanding spectacular views of the sea.

Once outside, walk down the hill, turn left and walk the few hundred metres to the **Oceanographic Institute** (open daily 6am–6pm; fee), the large French colonial building on your left. Founded in the 1920s, this was recently restored and will take less than 30 minutes to tour. Turtles, horseshoe crabs, lionfish and other denizens of the deep are pickled for posterity here while some of their relatives splash around in tanks outside.

Continue to **Cau Da village** 200m (220yds) further on and turn right into the port. On the way, you will see a wide display of shell paraphernalia: necklaces, watches, cigarette holders – you name it, Cau Da vendors can make it.

Vietnam's Foreign Pioneer

Take a *cyclo* to the **Pasteur Institute**, 10 Tran Phu Street (Mon–Fri 8–11am and 2–4.30pm; admission fee) and wait for an escort to guide you through its museum. Dr Alexander Yersin (1863–1943), perhaps the greatest foreign pioneer in Vietnam, spent 50 years in Nha Trang. A Frenchman of Swiss extraction, he was Louis Pasteur's most brilliant student and spent much of his life eradicating the plague bacteria from Southeast Asia. In the **Yersin**

Above: view from Bao Dai Villas

Museum you will see pictures of wooden houses being burnt to rid them of plague-ridden rats. Yersin also introduced rubber and quinine-producing trees to Vietnam. A veritable one-man wonder, Yersin taught himself the Vietnamese language, took mesmerizing photographs of the countryside and undertook three substantial explorations into the hinterland. On one of these, Yersin stood at Suoi Vang in Da Lat and noted in his diary that the area would make a pleasant hill station. His subsequent letter to Governor Doumer led to the founding of Da Lat.

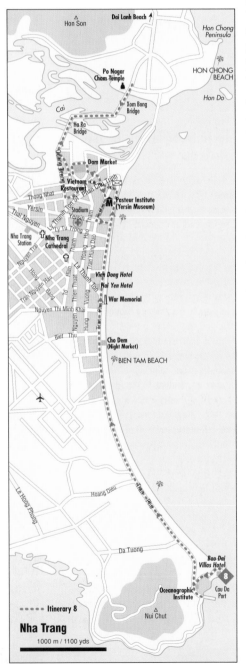

Walk down the beach and into town towards the **Dam Market** (open daily 7.30am–4.30pm) where you can find all kinds of souvenirs. For lunch, go to **Le Loi Street** and **Hoang Van Thu Street** where there is a group of restaurants specialising in *nem nuong*, one of the most delicious pancake-style foods that the locals eat. Look bewildered and the waiter will show you how to pile heaps of lettuce onto rice paper, then raw garlic, sliced shrimp roll, barbecued mince meat and green mango slices and then roll the whole thing.

Cham Culture

Depending on the weather and your energy level, either visit the Cham temple of **Po Nagar** and go to the beach later, or vice versa. If you decide on the first option, take a *cyclo* to visit Vietnam's oldest civilisation at Po Nagar (Thien Y-A-Na, Mother of the Kingdom) and one of the best preserved of Vietnam's ancient Cham culture remains. Set at the southern border of the greatest of the Cham kingdoms, Po Nagar represents the Goddess Uroja. Only four of the original eight towers remain, the tallest standing at a height of 5m (17ft). These were built between the 7th and 9th century

on a small hill north of the city. Following the precepts of Cham cosmology, the towers were also set on the banks of the Cai River, its waters symbolising fertility. You may still see flowers and incense burning in front of the phallic *linga* in the main tower, offerings from Cham people living nearby.

Choice Beaches and Diving

For beaches, you are spoiled for choice. You could go to the main **Nha Trang Beach**, or continue north past Po Nagar to the **Hon Chong Peninsula**, only 10 minutes away by *cyclo*, where a series of good beaches are found. The former is good for people-watching and facilities such as massages and snacks, and the latter for peace and quiet. The best beach, however, is at **Dai Lanh**, 85km (53 miles) away or an hour north by road through very picturesque scenery. You could hire a taxi and make a day trip to this stunning white-sand beach fringed with mountains and windswept pine trees.

The waters around Nha Trang are ideal for snorkelling and diving but take note that the rainy months are from October to mid-January. If you plan to dive, contact **Rainbow Divers** (90A Hung Vuong, tel: 058-524 351; www.divevietnam.com) led by a Briton, Jeremy Stein. Water visibility is good and excellent dive sites like Madonna Rock, Moray Beach and the Rainbow Reef are all within easy reach by boat.

For dinner, you could try Cho Dem or the **Night Market** (open daily 6–11pm), which lies across from 98 Tran Phu. Here a number of cafés serve some of the best seafood on the beach. After dinner, stroll down the beach to **Vien Dong Hotel** (tel: 058-821 606), 1 Tran Hung Dao Street, where there is a cultural show nightly from 7.30–9pm.

Above: fun on Nha Trang beach
Right: fishing boats at Cau Da port

The
Central Coast

This is Central Vietnam, with a flavour all of its own and distinct from Vietnam's extremities. Hoi An, the ancient cosmopolitan melting pot, so utterly different from anywhere else in Vietnam; Danang with its attractive waterfront and future as a communications centre; and Hue, the restful home of emperors' palaces and tombs, are all far from the seething masses of Ho Chi Minh City and the dilapidated grandeur of Hanoi.

One of the highlights of this area is the picturesque coastal drive across the spectacular Hai Van Pass between Danang and Hue. The road winds alongside the railway track and the Truong Son mountain range, climbing to an altitude of 1,000m (3,280ft), and affording startling vistas of mountain and deep blue sea. Between Danang and Hoi An are the Marble Mountains, a religious centre for the Chams as well as a haven for the Viet Cong during the war.

Although Danang is efficiently linked by transport because of its importance as a commercial centre – there are daily flights from Ho Chi Minh City, Hanoi and Nha Trang, and also bus and rail links between Danang and the major towns – I recommend that you stay in Hoi An, 32km (20 miles) south of Danang and easily accessed by road from the latter. Alternatively, stay at Cua Dai Beach, just 5 km (3 miles) from Hoi An. The gently sloping white sand beach is an attractive base and is currently seeing the construction of several beachside hotels. Hoi An is so special it demands to be viewed as a sort of Vietnamese Venice. The old port of Faifo was built on the water's edge, but the river receded over the centuries leaving this unique town untouched by development. Because the town is so small, in a few years it will seem as crowded as the Piazza San Marco on a summer's day. Now is the time to visit Hoi An.

Southwest of Hoi An is My Son, once capital of the Kingdom of Champa which flourished in this region centuries ago. And further south, ancient Cham towers dot the coast to as far as Qui Nhon and beyond; the drive along this stretch is a rewarding trip into Indochina's remote past.

To the north of Danang, accessed either by road via the scenic Hai Van Pass or by rail, is the city of Hue. The former capital and its Nguyen Tombs are redolent of the nation's imperial past and also speak volumes about Vietnam's love-hate relationship with China, its mighty neighbour to the north. The Imperial City was unashamedly and admiringly modelled upon the Forbidden City in Beijing, and even today the similarities are immediately apparent.

Note: the itineraries here assume you will fly to Danang, stay in Hoi An in the south and then make your way north to Hue. But you easily reverse the order by flying to Hue (served by thrice-daily flights on Vietnam Airlines) and then make your way south.

Left: interior of a Marble Mountain cave
Right: a tomb guardian in Hue

9. DANANG AND HOI AN *(see map, p49 & 50)*

Visit the remarkable Cham Museum in Danang, then head south, travelling past scenic Marble Mountains and China Beach to Hoi An, Vietnam's most delightful town. Lunch on the Vietnamese speciality 'cao lau' and then stroll round the exquisite old port of Faifo, visiting the Japanese Covered Bridge and some charming old houses.

Danang's **Cham Museum** (open daily 8am–5pm; admission fee) on the corner of Bach Dang and Tran Phu streets is Vietnam's finest museum, worth seeing for the building alone. It was built by the Ecole Francaise Extreme d'Orient in 1915 as an open-plan, colonial structure embellished with Cham-inspired motifs. The museum is laid out both methodically and aesthetically with

each room dedicated to a different Cham era, which in total spans over 1,000 years.

The museum contains the greatest display of Cham artefacts in the world, the Musee Guimet in Paris housing the next largest collection. You will see the deity Ganesh with his elephant head, Shiva dancing in his warlike manner, Nandin the bull mount of Shiva and many other figures, all sensuously erotic and finely carved. Buy the useful booklet (*Museum of Cham Culture – Danang*, Foreign Languages Publishing House, Hanoi, 1987) written by the museum curator, Tran Ky Phuong, on sale at the entrance. The Songhan floating restaurant on the Han River just opposite the Cham Museum makes an excellent venue for lunch – the seafood is both plentiful and delicious.

Marble Mountains, or Ngu Hanh Son, lie half way between Danang and Hoi An, about 15 minutes by car along National Highway 1. Marble from here was used in the construction of Ho Chi Minh's tomb in Hanoi (*see page 64*), a fact the locals are fiercely proud of. The mountains were a haven for the Viet Cong during the war as they overlooked the vast airforce base used by the Americans. Each of the five mountains is associated with one of the five elements, namely fire, water, earth, wood and metal. The largest mountain is home to several caves, some of which were used as Buddhist sanctuaries and even a Viet Cong hospital. Take the second entrance on your left as you walk towards the beach. **Huyen Khong Cave** – a Buddhist sanctuary which served as a Viet Cong base is the most spectacular. The highest cave, **Van Thong**, has a narrow passage through which you can wiggle to the top for the breathtaking views.

Bai Tam Non Nuoc, more popularly known as **China Beach**, a few minutes away, was where US marines once surfed in full view of the Viet Cong. Today it's making quite a comeback, and is ideal for a dip and a quiet rest under a beach umbrella. It's safe to delay your departure until quite late in the afternoon, as Hoi An is just a short drive away.

Above: Cham Museum in Danang

Delightful Hoi An

The small but historic town of **Hoi An**, located on the Thu Bon River 30km (18 miles) south of Danang, holds far more appeal than its big northern neighbour. During the time of the Nguyen lords and even under the first Nguyen emperors, Hoi An – then known as Faifo – was an important port, visited regularly by ships from Europe and all over the East. By mid-19th century, however, the progressive silting of the Thu Bon River and the development of nearby Danang combined to make Hoi An into a backwater, both literally and figuratively. The result is a delightful old town with many historical monuments – a place where the visitor may profitably linger and explore for several days. If you're hungry after that drive from Danang, go first to **Trung Bac Restaurant** (tel: 0510-864 622) at No. 87 Tran Phu Street and try *cao lau*, Hoi An's speciality. This is a noodle dish eaten with verbena, pork and rice pancakes.

Hoi An is today a UNESCO World Heritage Site (www.hoianworldheritage.org). An admission ticket of 75,000 dong gains you entry to all its old streets, one each of the three museums and assembly halls, one of the four old houses, and a music performance. The sights are open daily from 7am to 6pm.

Three streets delineate the old port of Faifo. Well-pre-

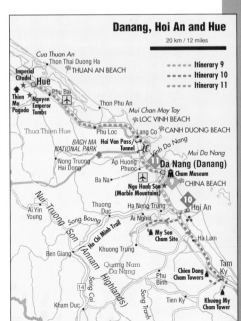

Danang, Hoi An and Hue

20 km / 12 miles

- - - - Itinerary 9
- - - - Itinerary 10
- - - - Itinerary 11

Cua Thuan An
Thon Thai Duong Ha
THUAN AN BEACH
Imperial Citadel
Hue
Phu Bai
Thon Phu An
Thien Mu Pagoda
Nguyen Emperor Tombs
Mui Chan May Tay
LOC VINH BEACH
Thua Thien Hue
Phu Loc
Lang Co
CANH DUONG BEACH
BACH MA NATIONAL PARK
Hai Van Pass/ Tunnel
Vinh Da Nang
Nong Truong Hai Dong
Ap Huong Phuoc
Da Nang (Danang)
Mui Da Nang
Cham Museum
Ba Na
Ngu Hanh Son (Marble Mountains)
CHINA BEACH
Nui Truong Son
Thuong Duc
Ha Nong Trung
Hoi An
Ai Yin Young
Song Boung
Ai Nghia
My Son Cham Site
Ha Lam
Ho Chi Minh Trail
Khuong Trung
Ben Giang
Quang Nam Da Nang
Chien Dang Cham Towers
Tam Ky
Song Cai
Phu Binh
Kham Duc
Song Tranh
Tien Ky
Khuong My Cham Tower
(Annam Highlands)
14

Above: Hoi An, the historic town

served houses – many of which are historical monuments – constructed from the wood of the jackfruit tree show the influences of foreigners on the trading post.

After lunch, walk down Tran Phu Street towards the market passing the **Quan Thang House** at No. 77. Dating back to the early 18th century, look out for its finely carved wooden walls enclosing the open courtyard.

Further down Tran Phu Street at No. 46 is the ornate **Fujian Assembly Hall**, which was built in 1757. Its elaborate triple-arched gateway, however, was built in 1975. Inside is an altar to Thien Hau, the deity who looks after fishermen and sailors. Look out also for the mural of the fathers of the original six Fujian families who sailed to Hoi An from China in the 17th century.

Further down Tran Phu Street at No. 24, on the corner by the market, is **Quan Cong Temple**, also called **Chua Ong**. Inside the temple, built in 1653, is a large papier-mâché statue of Quan Cong flanked by his general Chau Xuong and the mandarin Quan Binh. If there is time, visit the **Hoi An Museum of History and Culture** at the back (No. 7 Nguyen Hue Street) where precious artefacts documenting the history of Hoi An are displayed. The museum actually occupies the grounds of the **Quan Yin Pagoda**.

Now walk down through the market to the edge of the Thu Bon River and along Bach Dang Street to the city's most well known sight, the **Japanese Covered Bridge**. On the way, make dinner reservations at No 52, the **Café des Amis** (tel: 0510-861 360) for simple but tasty Vietnamese fare.

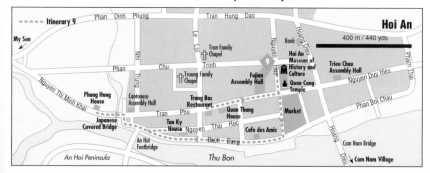

For years, the wooden Japanese Covered Bridge has drawn visitors to the carved dogs and monkeys guarding its entrances and restrained wooden panels. Japanese traders funded the building of this bridge during the 16th century and it was intended to perform a supernatural task. The Japanese believed that a great monster, living under the earth and stretching from India to Japan, caused earthquakes and destruction in their homeland by lashing its tail whenever it was angry. Building the bridge supposedly killed the monster by stabbing it in the heart.

The nearby 18th-century **Phung Hung House** (No. 4 Nguyen Thi Minh Khai Street) has been home to traders in perfumed woods and spices from the Central Highlands for several generations. Supported by hardwood columns, the architecture shows both Chinese and Japanese influences.

Double back pass the Japanese Covered Bridge to 101 Nguyen Thai Hoc Street to visit one of Hoi An's gems, the **Tan Ky House**. Seven generations have lived here, loving custodians of the beautiful wooden carvings that panel the house, now a museum. The house backs onto the water, where the original owner would have received his goods from traders plying the waters in the old days. Look for the elegant 'crab shell' ceiling and the exquisite mother-of-pearl inlay Chinese poetry hanging from the columns. You will see two badge-like objects adorning the top of many doors in Hoi An houses. These represent the forces of *yin* and *yang*, reflecting the influence of the over 50,000 ethnic Chinese living in Hoi An today. These watchful eyes also guard the house from evil spirits.

Then, have your long-awaited dinner at **Café des Amis**. Seafood is the speciality here, so ask for the catch of the day to go with its homemade wine.

10. MY SON AND CHIEN DANG *(see map, p49)*

The trip to historic My Son with its ancient Cham ruins is a journey back in time. For over a millennium, this region belonged to the Chams, a seafaring people who founded a great Hindu civilisation.

Start early for **My Son**. From Hoi An, take National Highway 1 south for 27km (16 miles) towards Tam Ky. Turn right at the sign to My Son and fork left after 9km (5½ miles). This journey should take less than an hour from National Highway 1. If coming from Danang, allow 30 minutes more for the journey to Hoi An.

Skirting the sacred **Cat's Tooth Mountain**, My Son (meaning Good Mountain) is probably the most important example of Cham architecture in Vietnam today. The My Son ruins, rust-coloured islands in a verdant sea of myrtle and other vegetation, are all that remains of the ancient religious capital of Amaravati, the greatest of the Cham states.

Ancient Champa

The Kingdom of Champa was established in or around the 2nd century, and for about 1,000 years (5th–15th century) it flourished in this region of Vietnam. At its

Left: the 16th-century Japanese Covered Bridge
Right: Cham sculpture

apogee, Champa controlled the entire central coast of what would later become Vietnam, from the Hoanh Son Pass in the north to the region of Vung Tau in the south. The Chams soon became Hinduised through commercial contacts with India, and their country functioned as a rather loose confederation of five states named after regions of India— Indrapura (Quang Tri), Amaravati (Quang Nam), Vijaya (Binh Dinh), Kauthara (Nha Trang) and Panduranga (Phan Rang).

At the start of the 10th century, Champa came under severe pressure from Dai Viet which was beginning its long push to the south. In 1069, Indrapura was lost to the Viets, and by 1306, Champa's northern frontier had been pushed back to the Hai Van Pass with the loss of Amaravati. The process of Vietnamese expansion proved inexorable, with Vijaya falling in 1471 and Champa – now reduced to the rump kingdoms of Kauthara and Panduranga – effectively a broken power. The final absorption by Vietnam was delayed until the reign of Minh Mang in 1832, by which time the victorious Vietnamese were already engaged in the conquest of the lower Cambodian regions of Prey Nokor (later renamed Saigon) and the Mekong Delta.

Champa disappeared – but not the Cham people. As their kingdom was swallowed piecemeal by Vietnam, increasing numbers of Cham fled to neighbouring Cambodia, though others chose to remain under Vietnamese tutelage in their former homelands. Today, there are as many as 500,000 'Western Chams' in Cambodia, nearly all of whom adopted Islam centuries ago. In Vietnam, the 'Eastern Chams' are fewer in number – perhaps 150,000 – and are divided between the Mekong Delta, where they are predominantly Muslim, and the central coast between Phan Rang and Phan Thiet (formerly Panduranga) where they are mainly Hindu. The artistic and religious legacy of Champa have survived all along the central coast of Vietnam, from Danang almost to Saigon, making an exploration of this region especially rewarding.

My Son's Monuments

The Cham people worshipped a dual cosmology, venerating both male and female deities. In Amaravati, My Son represented the male God king, denoted by the holy Cat's Tooth Mountain and a phallic representation, the *linga* Bhadresvarain. 'Bhad' is an abbreviation of Bhadravarman, an early Cham king, and 'esvara' refers to Lord Shiva.

Correspondingly, Po Nagar (*see page 44*) praised the female Goddess of the kingdom, Uroja, meaning breast. She is symbolized by nipples and breasts, which proliferate in traditional Cham sculpture, and the areca tree, signifying motherhood and fertility. The Chams re-created their own cosmos

Above: phallic *linga* at My Son with Cat's Tooth Mountain in the background
Right: carving of *Apsaras* at Chien Dang

at My Son. From a larger perspective, the Cat's Tooth Mountain was seen as the symbolic link between earth and heaven, an earthly *linga*, while the nearby river represented female fertility.

The temples of Champa generally follow one basic design. They represent Mount Meru, the Hindu abode of the gods, and generally face east towards the rising sun. The sanctum sanctorum – *kalan* in Cham – normally had a Shivalinga at its centre. Temples usually had three storeys and were plain inside. The structures were built first, then ornamented and fired by burning wood around them for days, creating a huge outdoor kiln. A wood glue was used as cement and gold was occasionally plastered on the rooftops. The outer walls, brick and sandstone, were carved with magnificent skill after construction had been completed.

As you walk among these ancient structures, imagine them during their heyday, decorated with colourful flags and alive with the humming of monks' incantations. At the height of the Champa kingdom, only a handful of attendants would have resided here, leaving the area a place of quiet mysticism for the gods to live in. Take your time to drink in the atmosphere. My Son was not always the sea of calm it is today. During the Second Indochina War (1954–75), the Viet Cong used this area as a base, causing the US airforce to strafe the ruins. As a result, many of the buildings, having survived the ravages of nature for centuries before, were summarily obliterated. Traces of around 70 temples and related structures may still be found at My Son, though only about 20 are still in good condition.

More Cham Relics

Leave My Son around midday and head south along Highway 1 towards Qui Nhon. The coast of Central Vietnam is studded with Cham towers from here south to Phan Rang. Near **Tam Ky**, the capital of Quang Nam province just 62km (39 miles) south of Danang, three Cham towers dating from the 11th century rise from a walled enclosure at **Chien Dang**. Here, there are fine sculptures of creatures from Hindu mythology – *naga, kinnaree, garuda, hamsa* and *makara* – as well as more mundane images of dancers, musicians and elephants. Also near Tam Ky is the important Cham site of **Khuong My**, a 10th-century temple complex renowned for its rich architecture.

Return to Hue or Danang if you have had your fill of ancient Cham culture. For those with time, continue down Route 1 south of Tam Ky pass **Quang Ngai** and **My Lai** – site of the massacre of Vietnamese civilians by US forces in 1968 – and on to **Qui Nhon**, 156km (98 miles) away. Spend the night at Qui Nhon, where there are simple accomodations, and visit more Cham monuments the next day at **Duong Long**, **Cha Ban** and **Thap Doi**.

11. ACROSS THE HAI VAN PASS TO HUE *(see map, p49)*

Take the Hai Van Pass for a breathtaking mountain descent and views of the sea before a leg-stretch and seafood lunch at idyllic Lang Co beach. Spend a relaxing afternoon swimming and sunning on the sands of Lang Co before heading out to Hue.

Before the opening of the **Hai Van Tunnel**, which carved 20km (12 miles) and 1 hour off the original trip, the wheezing buses laboured over the **Hai Van Pass**, or 'Pass Where the Clouds Meet the Sea', so-called because the 500-m (1,640-ft) high pass is often swathed in clouds and mist. Few tours use this route nowadays, but if possible, you should still venture over the

pass, for you will be rewarded with fantastic views. To climb the hill, you can hire a car – or, for even greater excitement, a motorbike taxi.

It takes about 3 hours to travel from Danang to Hue over the pass and in good weather the drive is out-standingly beautiful. If coming from Hoi An, it will take 30 minutes more, passing China Beach *(see page 48)* and picturesque Marble Mountains (Ngu Hanh Son). Make arrangements to rent a car and book accom-modations in Hue before you go. Take a swimsuit if it is a hot day and you plan to swim.

In the 15th century, the pass marked the boundary between the ancient Kingdom of Champa and Viet-nam. While less high and spectacular than the Ngoan Muc Pass between Da Lat and Phan Rang, the moun-tain descent along the Hai Van Pass affords a breath-taking view of the blue South China Sea.

When it's clear weather, the drive is simple enough – but when the pass is enveloped in clouds, watch out for slower vehicles. The summit of the pass is marked by an old French fort which often appears fleetingly through the swirling mist and clouds.

Note: This central coast area is notorious for changeable weather and you can expect temperature changes along the Hai Van Pass. The best sea-son is between January and May.

Idyllic Lang Co

Lang Co, a sleepy fishing village north of Hai Van Pass is the perfect place for lunch. Try the **Sao Bien Restaurant**, one of a string of restaurants just off the highway. The giant clams are excellent, as are grilled squid (*muc*

nuong) and fish soup. If you feel like a walk on the beach or a quick swim, drive over the Phuc Gia Pass and turn right after 2km (1¼ miles). **Loc Vinh Beach** is on your left after a further 4km (2½ miles). This idyllic stretch of beach will be the quietest and most stunning on your journey. The water is shallow near the beach and perfect for paddling in.

Beyond Lang Co, the road climbs over a low range of hills and then runs parallel to the Cau Hai and Thuy Tu lagoons, both home to tens of thousands of seabirds. Continue on to Hue for the night, a further 70km (43 miles), one hour by car. For dinner go to the **Huong Giang Hotel** (tel: 054-822 122) at 51 Le Loi Street. Overlooking the Perfume River, it has an excellent terrace restaurant where you can dine outdoors.

12. IMPERIAL HUE *(see map, p56)*

Hue, right in the centre of Vietnam, is known for its white lotuses, kings' tombs and the country's most beautiful girls. See the atmospheric Imperial Citadel, then cruise down the Perfume River for a tour of the ancient pagodas and imperial tombs of the Nguyen emperors.

Go to a kiosk on Le Loi Street on the southeast side of Phu Xuan Bridge and arrange for a boat to pick you up at about 11am by the bridge. Then go on a morning tour of the **Imperial Citadel** (open daily 7am–5pm). To get there, take a *cyclo* or walk to the north side of the Perfume River over the Phu Xuan Bridge. Turn left on Le Duan Boulevard and right over the citadel moat, then left to reach the **Noon Gate**, or Ngo Mon, which you will see towering above you.

The Imperial Citadel is a small city, now in its twilight years. Hue was badly damaged during the Second Indochina War, mostly during the 1968 Tet Offensive. For 25 days, the Viet Cong flag flew on the historic flagpole at the Flag Tower

Above: Lang Co beach
Right: canon at Flag Tower

(Cot Co). By the time its tattered remnants were lowered, nearly 10,000 people had died and Vietnam had lost much of its Imperial Citadel from where the Nguyen kings had ruled for over 100 years.

Emperor Gia Long, the first emperor (1802–19) of the Nguyen dynasty, a period generally regarded as the golden age of Vietnamese history, began to build the citadel in 1804. He was inspired by Vauban, France's great military architect, and created a citadel containing two cities, the Imperial City and the Forbidden Purple City. Stylistically, its design was a reasonably faithful copy of the Imperial City in Peking (Beijing). A geomancer was consulted over every aspect of the citadel; and every gate, lintel and pillar has a special significance.

Exploring the Imperial Citadel

The entrance to the **Imperial City** is called the Noon Gate because the sun, representing the emperor, is at its highest at noon. The Noon Gate, which you will enter, faces south and is therefore associated with prosperity. The guides from the Hue Monument Conservation Centre speak reasonably good English and are knowledgeable. The **Five Phoenix Tower**, found on top of the Noon Gate, was the setting for Emperor Bao Dai's abdication in 1945.

From the Noon Gate, proceed between placid lotus-filled ponds to the

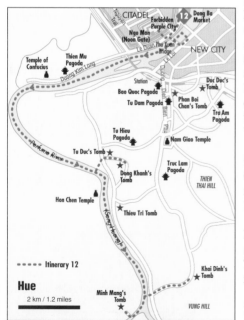

throne room in **Thai Hoa Palace**. Lotus flowers in Vietnam are usually pink, but in Hue they are white, a Buddhist symbol of purity. If you are unsure whether a pond flower is a lotus or water lily, just look at the leaves. Water lilies rest their leaves on the water's surface whereas lotus flower leaves point out to the sky. You will see both in Hue.

Thai Hoa Palace was the most important building in the Imperial City and this was where the emperor received important dignitaries of the land and foreign diplomats.

Beyond this, the **Forbidden Purple City** or Tu Cam Thanh stood until the 1968 Tet Offensive. Today, the city is slowly being rebuilt. Go west along the path,

Above: Imperial City gateway
Right: inside the Forbidden Purple City

paved so that Emperor Khai Dinh (1916–25) could drive his motor car here. Turn left to enter the **Hung Mieu** and **The Mieu** compound, a walled enclosure containing 10 shrines dedicated to Nguyen kings, as well as nine pot-bellied dynastic urns standing 2m (6½ft) tall, cast in 1822 and ornamented with motifs of the sun, moon, clouds, birds, animals, dragons, mountains, rivers, historic events and scenes from everyday life. Emperor Gia Long's urn is the most impressive and occupies a central position; another has bullet holes in it. There are all sorts of unlikely stories that the urns were created to boil the enemies of the emperor.

The **Museum of Royal Fine Arts** (open daily 7am–5pm; admission fee), formerly known as the Imperial Musuem, was built in 1845 under Thieu Tri. Located outside the East Gate of the citadel, the museum houses a collection of imperial clothing and furniture. Although a good number of the artefacts were either destroyed or lost during the revolution and war, some of the items are still worth seeing. Inscribed on the walls of the museum are poems written in ancient script.

Cast your imagination back to the time of the Nguyens. The life of a Nguyen emperor was reasonably relaxing. On a typical day, the emperor rose at 6am, filled in the Princes' Health Inquiry Card and devoted the morning to paperwork, attended by eunuchs and concubines. More serious emperors such as Minh Mang (1820–40) read books or composed poetry late into the night, and still found time for as many as five different concubines each night. The eunuchs kept a list of which night each concubine tended to the emperor in order to establish the legitimacy of the children born to them. Minh Mang sired 142 offspring during his time.

The Royal Court was run along even more complex lines than Versailles, with a similar amount of decorum and intrigue. Kings, concubines, eunuchs, queens and servants all lived to rigid protocol. Even the emperor's food was prepared with great ceremony. Clay pots used to prepare the food could only be used once, and as many as 50 dishes were cooked for one meal. The Nguyens drank *ruou thuoc*, an alcoholic drink with herbs to strengthen themselves. Old men in cafés around Hue still drink this potion today.

Perfume River

When you're done contemplating the lives of the Nguyens, take a *cyclo* to Dong Ba market to buy a picnic lunch. Then go back to Phu Xuan Bridge where you made arrangements for the boat trip earlier. The ride on the serene **Perfume River** is the most romantic way of capturing ancient Hue – if you take it slowly and luxuriate in the opulence of the past. Take a bicycle along with you on the boat if you prefer to come back by road.

Scattered on the hillsides on either side of the Perfume River are numerous pagodas and seven imperial tombs of the Nguyen emperors. Although the dynasty produced 13 kings, only seven reigned until their deaths and are buried here. The tombs, while reflecting the personal tastes of each emperor, follow a general pattern. Each has a large courtyard with stone figures of mandarins, elephants and horses; a stele pavilion with an engraved biography of the deceased king; a temple where the deceased king and queen were worshipped and the royal belongings displayed; a pleasure pavilion; and houses for the emperor's concubines, servants and soldiers. A number of the tombs were destroyed in the wars and the following tour only stops at the more interesting ones.

Thien Mu Pagoda, your first stop, has played a vital role in Buddhism in Vietnam. Its famous Happiness and Grace Tower (Phuoc Duyen), built in 1844, has seven storeys reaching 21m (69ft) high and has become a symbol of Hue.

Top: Tu Duc's Tomb is one of the loveliest
Above: plying the Perfume River

During the 1960s, Thien Mu was the centre of anti-government discontent. In 1963, Venerable Thich Quang Duc, a monk from Thien Mu, martyred himself in Saigon by self-immolation, in defiance of President Diem. This and subsequent immolations helped oust the staunchly Catholic President Diem. The Austin Cambridge Venerable Thich drove to the site of the suicide is enshrined here. Pause for a moment as you return to your boat: the view along the Perfume River from Thien Mu is outstanding.

Tu Duc's tomb will be the first you come to, and you must disembark and walk (or cycle) a short distance. Tu Duc (1847–83) killed his elder brother to ascend to the throne in 1847. He spent considerable time and energy devising plans for his tomb, arguably the loveliest in Hue. Set in a 12-ha (29½-acre) garden, the tomb is surrounded by a wall. Overlooking a large lotus pond is a pretty pavilion where Tu Duc supposedly drank tea made from the dew of lotus flowers. All the workers associated with the tomb were executed so that nobody could desecrate it or discover the whereabouts of the treasure Tu Duc was buried with. The French however tried to exhume the body, as the uneven paving stones attest to.

About 500m (547yds) further down the road after Tu Duc's tomb lies **Dong Khanh's tomb**. Dong Khanh (1885–89) was the nephew and adopted son of Tu Duc. His is the smallest of the imperial tombs but also one of the most unusual because of its two separate sections. This tomb was featured in the film *Indochine* and is now under renovation.

Return to your boat and bypass the Hon Chen temple to the furthest point in your journey, **Minh Mang's tomb**, about 12km (7½ miles) from the city and considered to be the most utopian spot in Hue. Minh Mang (1820–40) was a disciplined Confucian and one of the greatest Nguyen rulers. Three red gates lead to the Honour Courtyard, and if you continue up to the **Lake of Impeccable Clarity** you'll see an inspiring pavilion at the top, a good spot to stop and take in the atmosphere.

If you're returning by boat, just relax and enjoy the view. If you're going back by road, go via **Khai Dinh's tomb** (1916–25), the last Nguyen emperor to be buried here. The architectural style of this ferro-concrete tomb reflects the conflicting influences of Khai Dinh's time. A host of mandarins line the courtyard in stony silence, guarding a French-inspired interior. The tomb, while impressive in a rather gaudy way, is also strangely symbolic of Nguyen dynasty corruption and decline. Khai Dinh, not to mention his successor Bao Dai, were almost as French as they were Vietnamese, and the downfall of their dynasty was clearly inevitable in this proudly nationalistic land.

Right: tomb of Khai Dinh

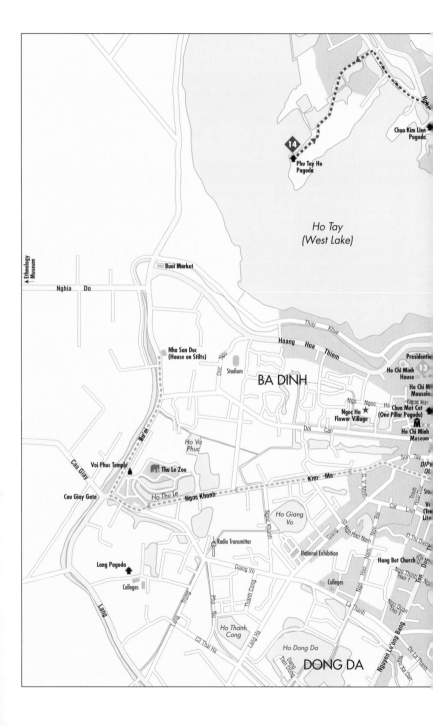

Chua Kim Lien
Pagoda

14

Phu Tay Ho
Pagoda

*Ho Tay
(West Lake)*

Buoi Market

▲ Ethnology
Museum

Nghia Do

Thuy Khue

Hoang Hoa Thiem

Nha San Duc
(House on Stilts)

Dao Tan

Stadium

BA DINH

Presidenti

Ho Chi Minh
House

13

Ho Chi M
Mausole

Ngo Ngoc Ha

Ngoc Ha ★
Flower Village

Chua Mot Cot
(One Pillar Pagoda)

Ho Chi Minh
Museum

Doi Can

Buoi Tan

Ho Va
Phuc

Cau Giay

Voi Phuc Temple

Thu Le Zoo

Son Tay

DIP
QU

Kim Ma

Cau Giay Gate

Ho Thu Le

Ngoc Khanh

Ngo Khanh

Ho Giang
Vo

Giang Vo

Ngo Hao Nam

Cat Linh

Trinh
Hoai Duc

Sta

Vo
(Tem
Lite

O Thi Dien

Radio Transmitter

National Exhibition

Hang Bot Church

Hao Thinh
Hao 1

Ngo
Duc

Lang Pagoda

Giang Vo

Colleges

Colleges

Ngo Quan
Tho

La Thanh

Nguyen Luong Bang

De La Thanh

Ngo Xa Dan

Lang

Lang Trung

Phu Nu

Thanh Cong

Lang Ha

C2 Thai Ha

Dang Tien Dong

Ho Thanh
Cong

Ho Dong Da

DONG DA

Hanoi

1000 m / 1100 yds

----- Itinerary 13
━━━ Itinerary 14

Song Hong (Red River)

GIA LAM

gu Xa Pagoda
ruc
ch
ite
ake)

Ngu Xa

Kon Phu

P. P. Duc Chinh

Pham Hong Thai

Nguyen Truong To

Hang Than

Hong Nhai

Hoe Nhai Pagoda

Long Bien Bridge

Nguyen Van Cu

Chuong Bridge

anh Temple
hanh
ium

Phan

Dinh

Phung

P. Cang Dung

P. Phuong

Thu

Pagoda

CITADEL

Heavenly Palace

Hanoi Ancient Capital

Flag Tower

Vietnam Military
History Museum

Lenin Statue

Cao
Ba Quat

Tran Thi

Cafe
252

Nam De

Cua
Dong

Hang De

Phung

Hung

OLD QUARTER

H. Chieu

Dao

H. Khoai

Tran Nhat Duat

Phuc Tan

Bach Ma Temple

Buom

Cha Ca
La Vong

Chuong Vang Theatre

Ngoc Quyen

Hang Bac

87 Ma May

HOAN KIEM

Khaisilk

Thang Long Water Puppet Troupe
Shoe Market

Ngoc Son
Temple

Gia Ngu

Lo Su

Cau
Go

Ham Tu
Quan

Ho
Hoan
Kiem

Kim Dong Theatre

Ba Da Pagoda

Tran N. Han

Do

Chuong

St Joseph's
Cathedral

Main Post
Office

Le Lai

Le Thach

Revolution
Museum

National Library

H. Khay

19th
December
Market

Hai

Metropole
Hotel

Cong Nhan Theatre

History Museum

Municipal Theatre (former Opera House)

Quan Su
Pagoda

Ly

Thuong

Kiet

Hang

Bai

Trung

Geology
Museum

Cultural Palace

Tran Hung Dao

Police
Station

Pham Ngu Lao

oi Railway
Station

Le Duan

Yet Kieu

Tran Quoc Toan

Nguyen Du

Tran Nhan Tong

Ngo

Quan

Phan Chu Trinh

Ham Long

Mai Gallery

Tran Thanh Tong

Ho Thien
Quang

Nguyen Binh Khiem

Ba Trieu

Tuoi Tre
Theatre

Lo Duc

Tran Khanh

Du

Kim Lien
Bus Station

Circus Theatre

REUNIFICATION
PARK

Nha Hat Cheo
Theatre

Tran Xuan Soan

Dai Nam
Theatre

Hoa Ma

Song Hong (Red River)

Hanoi
& the North

Hanoi, the cultural and political capital of Vietnam, is also its most stylish city. French colonial architecture reached its zenith here, and there are few more golden memories than of walking around the backstreets of Hanoi in the evening, enjoying the faded elegance of the tree-lined boulevards and alleys. Both Vietnamese and foreigners delight in making comparisons between Hanoi and Ho Chi Minh City. Hanoi women, for instance, are prettier and noticeably taller than women in the south.

Just a few years ago, Hanoi had the feel of a university town. Today, the capital city is heading towards graceful maturity as Honda Dreams pack the streets of the Old Quarter and hotels sprout up. There are fewer direct international flights to Hanoi compared to Ho Chi Minh City but the situation is improving slowly. Internally, Hanoi is serviced by regular Vietnam Airlines flights to Ho Chi Minh City, Danang, Hue, Nha Trang, Ban Me Thuot, Da Lat, Dien Bien Phu, Pleiku, Phu Quoc and Qui Nhon.

Legends are inextricably woven into Hanoi's history. In 1010, Emperor Ly Thai To founded the city after seeing an auspicious Golden Dragon rise from the area. He dubbed his new capital Thang Long, or Ascending Dragon. Myths also surround the origins of the two main lakes, Ho Tay and Ho Hoan Kiem. Fables aside, the reality of Hanoi's development is a troubled one, from its origins on the geomancer's draughtboard to being usurped by Hue during the Nguyen dynasty, and its subsequent capture and colonisation by the French in 1882. In 1954, Hanoi, with a population of just 300,000, was declared the capital of the Democratic Republic of Vietnam. Nearly 20 years later, Operation Rolling Thunder, the world's first example of 'carpet bombing', destroyed a quarter of the city and threatened to wipe it off the map forever.

Today, over 3 million Hanoians are packed into the city. The capital of the Socialist Republic of Vietnam since 1976, Hanoi has ruled the reunified country with an increasingly soft hand as modernisation and a market economy begin to take shape. As Hanoi enters the 21st century, it is also becoming a Bohemian capital of the arts, with galleries and exhibitions mushrooming throughout the city.

Beyond Hanoi and its suburbs are picturesque provinces dotted with rice fields and pagodas. To the east is the UNESCO World Heritage Site of Halong Bay, with its mist-shrouded grottoes and jutting rocks while Sapa, the mountainous northern territory, near the Chinese border, is home to colourful indigenous tribes.

Left: breakfast along the streets of Hanoi
Right: contemporary soldiers in marching parade

13. HO CHI MINH MAUSOLEUM
AND THE OLD QUARTER *(see map, p60–1)*

Morning walking tour of Ho Chi Minh mausoleum, house and museum, followed by a Vietnamese buffet lunch. Afternoon visit to the 'House on Stilts', and a shopping spree in the Old Quarter. In the evening, settle back for a water puppet performance.

Rise early and go to 57 Dinh Tien Hoang Street, by Hoan Kiem Lake, to buy tickets for the 8pm performance of the **Thang Long Water Puppet Theatre** (they sell out later in the day). Take a *cyclo* or drive to **Ho Chi Minh Mausoleum** (Apr–Oct Tues–Thur 7.30–10.30am, Sat–Sun 7.30–11am; Nov–Mar Tues–Thur 8–11am, Sat–Sun 8–11.30am; free) at 8 Hung Vuong Street soon after opening if you intend to make it for the morning tour. Dress appropriately for the tour of the icy cold mausoleum complex, and as cameras are not permitted inside, don't forget to get yours back when you leave.

The mausoleum – with Ho Chi Minh's embalmed body as its star attraction – is Vietnam's most sacred secular building and symbolises the national struggle for a free Vietnam. Ho Chi Minh is unequivocally Vietnam's Ultimate National Hero. Acquainting yourself with his life and works is central to understanding the Vietnam of today, and you can't do better than to tour his mausoleum, the house where he lived and worked in the later years of his life, and the museum dedicated to him. The square in front of the mausoleum is where Ho Chi Minh made the declaration of Independence on 2 September 1945, now Vietnam's National Day.

A short walk from the mausoleum is **Ho Chi Minh House** (daily except Mon and Fri morning, Apr–Oct 7.30–11am, 2–4pm; Nov–Mar 8–11am, 1.30–4pm; admission fee) which he lived in the decade prior to his death in 1969. It is one of Hanoi's most peaceful spots. Note the former governor's residence and the pond as you enter the compound of this house built on stilts. Ho Chi Minh was known for living simply, but people often forget to add 'and tastefully'. The house – with Ho Chi Minh's books, typewriter, telephone and other artefacts – and surroundings have great charm.

Follow the path through the garden to **Chua Mot Cot** (One Pillar Pagoda). If time is short, tour the Ho Chi Minh Museum first because of its restricted hours and return here later. Scores of domestic tourists have their photographs taken in front of this pagoda, said to be credited with miraculous healing powers, built by Emperor Ly Thai To after he was inspired by a dream. The wooden original, dating from the 11th century, was destroyed at the end of the French colonial era and was rebuilt in 1955. If you visit on the first or 15th day of the lunar month, the adjacent **Duu Tien Pagoda** will be open.

Ho Chi Minh Museum (open daily

Right: cycling past Ho Chi Minh Mausoleum

8–11.30am and 2–4pm; admission fee), behind the mausoleum, was opened in 1990 with no expenses spared. Exhibits cover the early years of the young globetrotting Ho Chi Minh, his exile years, and his struggle against the French colonialists. Towards the end of the tour, the links between Ho Chi Minh and the displays grow somewhat tenuous, culminating in some strange Masonic imagery and rooms that resemble nuclear fission chambers. Still, the design of the museum alone with its state-of-the-art spatial images is worth seeing, the first of its kind in Vietnam.

When you are finished, hop on a *cyclo* past the diplomatic area just between Le Hong Phong and Tran Phu streets. Some of the most spectacular French colonial buildings are found in this area. Then, tell the driver to take you to 26 Nguyen Thai Hoc Street for lunch at **Brother's Café** (tel: 04-733 3866). A superb Vietnamese buffet is served in an attractive 19th-century colonial villa set in landscaped gardens. Authentic 'street' food as well as gourmet Vietnamese fare is served here. If the weather is nice, ask for one of the tables on the terrace.

Another House on Stilts

To get to **Nha San Duc** (open daily 8–11.30am and 1.30–4pm) at No 1 Vinh Phuc Street, another house on stilts, is relatively tricky. It is a 45-minute *cyclo* or 20-minute taxi ride away and your driver may not know the way. To get there, go down Kim Ma Street past the **Thu Le Zoo** on your right and turn right into Buoi Street. Head down this street until you see Ngo (Lane) 462 on your right. Go down this lane and take the first left turn. Just before No. 16 on your right is a small narrow alley: ask your driver to wait here. Walk down the alley – the stilt house you are looking for is immediately on your left as you exit the alley. Allow enough time to get lost.

Having seen the smart 1950s house on stilts that was Ho Chi Minh's, you now see the inspiration for it, albeit out of context. Duc, a renowned ceramic collector, bought this house from a Hmong tribesman in Hoa Binh province 30 years ago and transported it to its present site in Hanoi lock, stock and bar-

Above: Hanoi's old quarter

rel. The house brims with antiques as well as artefacts that are manufactured to look old. Many of the 'distressed' Buddhas on display are made at Duc's factory. Although a bit pricey, this is probably the most unusual souvenir shop in Vietnam. Keep an eye open for terracotta Chinese dolls houses, originally made to be buried with Chinese mandarins so that the latter would have a place to live in heaven.

On your way back from Nha San visit **Thu Le Zoo** (open daily, 6am–9pm) which has a small but interesting collection of birds, including silver pheasants, Siamese firebacks and Vo Qui pheasants.

Artisans' Village

Hop on a *cyclo* to Hanoi's **Old Quarter**, also known as the '36 Streets', a warren of former artisans' workshops located in an area to the north of Hoan Kiem Lake. Each street represents a guild or industry, for instance Votive Paper Street or Grilled Fish Street. **Hang Gai Street** is a mecca for lovers of silk, and also has some of the best embroidered-cotton shops in town. **Khaisilk** at No 96 is the finest silk shop in Vietnam. Khai buys his silk from a distant area of northern Vietnam so it differs slightly from his main rival, **Duc Loi Silk**, at No 102. While tailor-made clothes take only a few days to make, collect them a day or two before you leave in case you need last-minute alterations done.

Walk down Hang Gai Street towards Hoan Kiem Lake, taking Hang Dao Street left and turning right on Hang Buom Street. About 200m (218ft) on the left is the 9th-century **Bach Ma Temple** or White Horse Temple (open daily, 7.30–11am, 1.30–6pm), the Old Quarter's most revered and ancient place of worship. Its architecture is influenced by the Chinese community, and a magnificent red funeral palanquin serves as its highlight.

Aim to reach **Cha Ca La Vong** restaurant (tel: 04-825 3929) at 14 Cha Ca Street at 7pm and go upstairs if there is space for *cha ca,* the one and only dish served here. A brazier and various side dishes will be brought. Throw in the dill, the green part of the spring onions and the fish into the hot pan. In your eating bowl, put a portion of the white noodles, mint, peanuts, the white part of the spring onions, some fish sauce and the cooked fish on top. Alternatively, if the restaurant is full, try the same dish at the quieter **Cha Ca Thanh Long**, 31 Duong Thanh Street (tel: 04-824 5115).

Now walk to the **Water Puppet Theatre** at Dinh Tien Hoang Street. Sit back and enjoy perhaps the oldest indigenous form of entertainment in Vietnam. Wooden puppets manipulated by bamboo sticks, which are hidden beneath the water, play out stories based on Vietnamese fables as well as historical and daily events, accompanied by traditional music. The more expensive tickets include a free video tape of the performance as well as a nice memento. Imagine what it was like four centuries ago, when a troupe arrived in a far-off village and performed on the local duck pond.

14. CENTRE FOR ARTS *(see map, p60–1)*

Breakfast at Café 252, then walk to the Fine Arts Museum and Temple of Literature. After a 'bun cha' lunch, an afternoon tour of West Lake and its pagodas. In the early evening, walk around Hoan Kiem Lake, taking in the Metropole Hotel, the Opera House and Mai Art Gallery.

Go to **Café 252** at 252 Hang Bong Street for a relaxing breakfast. Pictures of Catherine Deneuve plaster the walls since the actress' visit during the filming of *Indochine*. The smoked ham is excellent. Proceed to the **Fine Arts Museum** at 56 Nguyen Thai Hoc Street (Tues, Thur, Fri and Sun, 8.30am–5pm; Wed and Sat 8.30am–9pm; admission fee), a beautiful building packed with fascinating artefacts. Get a guide if one is available. The museum was originally a French nunnery, converted in 1965 with Russian aid and Cham embel-

lishments, and now painted in muted tones to complement its contents. Towering in front of the main entrance is a huge Hindu phallic *linga*.

Go straight to the top floor. Some of the early 20th-century paintings on display here are highly regarded. The second floor is devoted to the costumes of ethnic minorities and objects from Vietnam's distant past.

Van Mieu, **The Temple of Literature** (open daily 8am–5pm; admission fee), is a few steps away in the square made by Nguyen Thai Hoc, Quoc Tu Giam, Hang Bot and Van Mieu streets. Go around the square to the entrance on the opposite (south) side. This is Vietnam's oldest university, dating from 1070 and founded by Emperor Ly Thanh Tong. Covering some 3ha (7½ acres), five interconnecting courtyards form the ground plan leading to the House of Ceremonies dedicated to Confucius. Inside, you

Right: Van Mieu, the Temple of Literature

will see the sage depicted with his four most studious pupils. Until 1802, when the temple functioned as a university, it was extremely difficult to become a mandarin and only an elite minority went on to certain fortune after a series of arduous triennial examinations. The typical mandarin hopeful would arrive with a bamboo pole slung across his shoulder, carrying books and a tent with

him on the long road to Hanoi. You can see one of these mobile libraries or *ganh* in the gallery to your right as you enter the Great Success Sanctuary. Students who achieved mandarinhood had their names displayed on a stele set on the backs of stone tortoises. These were restored in 1993 and tiled roofs now cover the stone tablets.

After a morning on your feet, relax over a *bun cha* lunch. This is a delicious lunchtime speciality of grilled pork served with a mountain of green herbs and cold noodles with fish sauce. Excellent *bun cha* places can be found at 61 Ly Thai Tho Street but especially good is the tiny outlet at 20 Ta Hien Street.

Picturesque Lakes and Pagodas

Organise a *cyclo* or a taxi for the next hour to see the east shore of **Ho Tay**, or West Lake. **Tran Quoc Pagoda** was moved here in the 17th century because of flood waters. The smaller lake, formed by the causeway, is called **Ho Truc Bach** (White Silk Lake). The Trinh lords built a palace here in the 18th century which was later turned into a reformatory for errant royal concubines. As punishment, they were condemned to weave a very fine white silk, hence the name. The shore of Ho Tay is now the scene of large-scale modern development. As you drive along Yen Phu Street, imagine what its 13-km (8-mile) circumference will look like in five years. Two pagodas on the shore of Ho Tay, **Chua Kim Lien** and **Phu Tay Ho**, down a long footpath, are worth stopping at for views of the lake.

Now go to **Ho Hoan Kiem**, the Lake of the Restored Sword. Legend has it that in the 15th century, King Le Loi, while he still was a humble fisher-

man, was presented with a magical sword by a giant tortoise living in the lake. He later used the sword to drive the Chinese from the country but eventually the sword was reclaimed by the tortoise. The three-tiered **Tortoise Pagoda** in the middle of the lake is dedicated to the mythical creature.

French Architecture

Walk down Trang Tien Street towards the **Opera House**. The magnificent facade of the French-designed building is still one of the grandest sights in Hanoi. It can be difficult to gain access into the recently restored interior during the day, but you might be lucky enough to catch a performance at night. This might be anything from the National Symphony Orchestra or visiting performers. Keep an eye on the notice board outside. You will pass several bookshops on your right. The alleys are especially interesting for photocopies of pirated books in English. To your left up Ngo Quyen Street is the **Sofitel Metropole**, the smartest hotel in Vietnam by a long way and where author Graham Greene stayed in the 1950s. Go inside to have a look at its renovated interior, still imbued with a French old world charm.

Just before you sneak off, exhausted, to take a shower, make a detour to **Mai Gallery**, at 3B Phan Huy Chu. Mai and her father, Duong Tuong, have on display some outstanding works, including a few by the so-called Gang of Five, a group of artists on the cutting edge of the recently liberated Hanoi arts scene, and paintings by Bui Xuan Phai, regarded as the father of contemporary art in Vietnam. Now take a cyclo to 11B Dien Bien Phu Street to enjoy Hanoi's finest pizza and pasta dishes at **Luna d'Autunno** (tel: 04-823 7338) alfresco style or in the covered restaurant area.

15. THE PERFUME PAGODA *(see map, p71)*

Day trip to the ethereal homeland of Buddhism in Vietnam, and the 'most beautiful grotto under the southern sky'.

Start early as you will be travelling 60km (37 miles) southwest of Hanoi. The journey comprises three parts: by road, by boat and a 4-km (2½-mile) hike. Most Hanoi tour operators *(see page 100)* run this tour with lunch, entrance fees, transport and guide included in the price: other attractions are sometimes visited en route.

During the first two months after Tet (roughly February/March or March/April depending on the lunar calendar), the Perfume Pagoda can get very crowded with pilgrims, making for a frustrating (or alternatively, highly interesting) experience. The walk up the mountain is steep and can be quite tough going so wear sensible shoes and bring a bottle of water. In the summer, it can get very hot and sweaty. Boats have no cover, so wear sun protection. As there are no places to eat along the way, bring a picnic lunch if your tour package does not include one, plus a torch for the caves.

The journey by road brings you to riverside **Duc**

Top Left: the Opera House **Left:** religious procession, Ho Hoan Kiem **Right:** carving at Perfume Pagoda

Khe village, where you board a shallow metal-bottomed boat (there are no roads to the Perfume Pagoda). For many, the 60-minute boat trip along the wide, swiftly flowing **Yen River** is almost as worthwhile as visiting the pagoda itself. Relax in your shallow metal boat as the oarsman steers you along the river and take in the surrounding landscape of jagged limestone hills.

Temples Galore

The site of the oddly misnamed **Perfume Pagoda** (open daily, 7.30am–6pm) comprises a group of temples covering an area of 30sq km (11⅙sq miles). Built into the limestone cliffs of the **Huong Tich Mountain** (Ancient Vestiges of Perfume Mountain), the earliest temples date from the 15th century; by the early 20th century there were over 100. This area was the site for some bitter uprisings against the French colonialists and as a result, several buildings were destroyed during the late 1940s. Fortunately, the area retains much of its natural splendour and is regarded as one of the most beautiful spots in Vietnam.

Disembark from the boat at the base of the Huong Tich Mountain for your 1½–2 hour hike or take the convenient cable car.

Thien Tru Temple or Heavenly Kitchen (a reference to a Vietnamese constellation, not to the secular noodle stalls that cluster around it) reaches up the mountain ahead. Recent restoration has left the complex with a guesthouse and a karaoke bar, thankfully only for use during the festival season. The path to the right of the temple leads to your destination 2km (1¼ miles) away. On your return, you may wish to climb the stone staircase to the right of the path leading to the **Tien Son Temple**, where there are unusual stone musical instruments made from stalagmites.

Ten minutes along the main path you will see a shrine built over a spring. Legend has it that if you bathe in **Giai Oan** your spirit will be purified and false charges against you cleared. You will see the shrine to **Cua Vong** (Goddess of the Mountains) where the path thins and becomes a little steeper. Your destination, the **Huong Tich Grotto**, lies just below the summit of this mountain. You will see the portal and 120 stone steps bedecked with Buddhist flags leading down to the grotto's smoky depths. Chinese characters etched on the outside of the cave in 1770 declare this to be the 'most beautiful grotto under the

Above: riding Yen River to the pagoda
Right: shrine at Perfume Pagoda

southern sky'. Through the haze of incense smoke you will see women with offerings of fruit and incense, as well as candles and noodles for hungry pilgrims. There can be few more uplifting sights than of solemn-faced pilgrims, candles clutched in their hands, treading the damp staircase to the shrine. Don't spoil the mood: use your torch only if you need to.

The huge stalagmites at the mouth of the cave bear curious names. The bulbous one in the centre is called the **Rice Stack**, while other stalagmites inside have been named the **Mountain of the Teenage Goddess**, **Silkworms Chamber**, **Cocoons Rack** and the **Heap of Coins**. The bell near the entrance dates from 1655 and is only beaten on ceremonial occasions. Romantically inclined Vietnamese compare the cave to a dragon's mouth, with the steps leading into the cavern as its throat.

As your eyes grow accustomed to the darkness you will see several altars twinkling with candlelight. The central one houses an important statue of **Quan Am** (Goddess of Mercy), the female personification of the Buddha. Her androgynous figure is swathed in a blue-green fabric. According to folklore, the *bodhisattva* Avalokiteshvara transformed himself into the female deity Quan Am here, and the shrine is dedicated to her.

For many Vietnamese this is the most important religious area in the whole of Vietnam and many devout Buddhists will try and visit the shrine at least once in their lives. It is said that the Buddha himself may have visited this area once, leaving his perfumed footprint, the first of many theories about the origins of the name 'Perfume'.

Today, monks conduct services at 4am, midday and 6pm, the pitter-patter of Buddhist drums keeping time with the sound of condensation droplets falling in the cave.

For your return journey, choose a nice spot on the boat to fully enjoy scenery that has inspired generations of Vietnamese poets and monks.

hanoi & the north

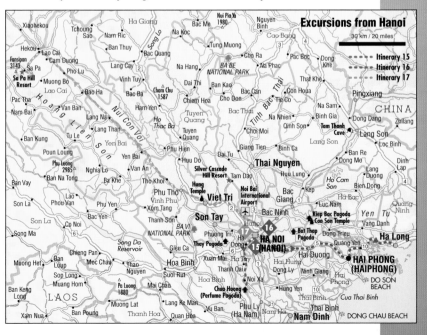

16. HALONG BAY *(see map, p71)*

A two-day trip to Vinh Ha Long, or Halong Bay, Vietnam's most famous natural marvel. Limestone outcrops jutting out from the sea form a picturesque scene at any time of the day. View the bay from a boat and soak in the timeless surroundings which have astonished sailors and inspired legends for centuries.

This is one destination where booking through a tour agency can really help. It's much cheaper and easier than to arrange things by yourself, especially as unscrupulous boat owners in Halong City are notorious for ripping off tourists. There are several options: A reliable mid-priced operator is **Handspan** (tel: 04-933 2375; www.handspan.com) on board its comfortable *Dragon's Pearl* Chinese junk; it also offers kayaking trips in the bay as an option. **Buffalo Tours** (tel: 04-828 0702; www.buffalotours.com) is another reputable company that operates a luxury junk with a kayak tour option. More expensive are boat tours by **Exotissimo** (tel: 04-828 2150; www.exotissimo.com) and **Emeraude** (tel: 04-934 0888; www.emeraude-cruises.com). The latter company uses a replica 19th-century French single-wheeled paddle steamer.

But first, you have to take the 165-km (103-mile) drive from Hanoi (about 3 hours) through Quang Ninh province to **Bai Chay** in Halong City, the jump-off point for your Halong Bay tour. It is almost impossible to visit Halong Bay as a day trip. There are one-day tours with roughly four hours cruising, but this is not worthwhile given the long road journey to Halong City.

The best time to visit Halong is in warmer weather, from April to October, as you can swim off the boat and relax on sundecks. However, during the peak typhoon season in August, boats may cancel due to bad weather. Between January and March, the weather can be cool and drizzly but even then Halong Bay is a worthwhile excursion: the swirling mists that swaddle the magnificent limestone outcrops (or karsts) lend an ethereal beauty to it.

There are certainly karst formations to be found elsewhere – Thailand's Phang Nga Bay for instance – but few travellers could fail to be impressed with Halong Bay, with more than 3,000 limestone islands jutting out of the emerald green waters in the Gulf of Tonkin.

In an area covering 1,500sq km (580sq miles), sampans, junks, fishing boats as well as numerous tourist boats – sail past a fairytale backdrop of mostly uninhabited limestone karsts, which yield numerous grottoes, secluded coves, coral beaches and hidden lagoons. It is no wonder then that UNESCO twice designated this area a World Heritage Site, first in 1994 for its outstanding natural scenic beauty, and again in the year 2000 for its great biological interest.

Left: mist-shrouded Halong Bay

Mythical Halong Bay

Halong Bay's rocky islands and outcrops form a natural stockade that has saved Vietnam from foreign enemies more than once. One of the more famous stories involves Ngo Quyen, who defeated the Chinese in 938 by booby-trapping the mouth of the Bach Dang River with iron-tipped stakes and then luring the Chinese up the river as the tide went out. Incredibly, four centuries later, Kublai Khan fell for the same trick, this time masterminded by Tran Hung Dao, whose statue you will see in many cities.

As you approach each jutting monolith in the bay, ponder how these strange islands and caves came to be. According to Vietnamese folk tradition, this is where a great dragon rushed headlong into the sea and came to a rather bumpy landing, tearing up the ground as it went and leaving the remains of the islands we see today.

Geologists believe that the karsts were formed by a great limestone seabed eroding until only the pinnacles remained behind. Elements within the rock were slowly dissolved by rain water, forming strangely shaped caverns that have spawned a host of legends and names: the **Virgin's Cave**, **Grotto of the Heavenly Palace**, the **Fighting Cocks**. **Hang Hanh Cave** which spans 2km (1¼ miles) is interesting for its fantastic rock formations.

Cat Ba Island

Cat Ba Island, the largest in Halong Bay at 354sq km (136sq miles) offers more spectacular landscape – forested limestone peaks, coral reefs, coastal mangrove and freshwater swamps, lakes and waterfalls. **Lan Ha Bay** on its eastern edge has particularly nice beaches to explore. Almost half the island and its adjacent waters are a national park, with diverse flora and fauna. Although the island is dotted with a few villages, most boats dock in the picturesque fishing harbour, where small hotels and tourist services are located. Although tourism plays an increasingly dominant role, Cat Ba is still a fishing community. Many tourist boats spend one or two nights here, or visit the national park.

Above: picture perfect Halong Bay

17. SA PA *(see map, p71)*

A trekking paradise unvisited by outsiders for half a century high up near the border with China. Explore emerald-green stepped hills and pine forests – home to brightly-dressed hilltribes. Enjoy Vietnam's most scenic rural spot over three or, better still, five days.

The best time to visit is September to November and March to May. The rainy summer months, particularly July and August, are Sapa's busiest months (with the most expensive hotel rates), when Hanoians flock here to escape the heat. Temperatures can plummet in winter, with frost and occasional snow, so be sure to book a room with heating if visiting during winter months. Nighttime temperatures are low throughout the year, so bring warm clothing. The weather, however, can be variable all year: blazing hot, then low cloud, rain and fog suddenly rolling in. Weekends – especially peak summer months – can get very crowded; weekdays are more relaxed, and with lower room rates.

Every Hanoi tour operator *(see page 100)* organises Sapa tours – from one to several nights – with guide, transport, accommodation and various tour options. Sapa, 360km (223 miles) northwest of Hanoi, is also one of the relatively few easy destinations for independent travellers, but be sure book your return train ticket in advance as weekends are busy. Night trains (soft-sleeper four-berths with fan or air-conditioning; for more comfort, opt for the Tulico berths, tel: 04-828 7806; www.tulico-sapa.com) depart daily from Tran Quy Cap station (behind the main station on Le Duan Street) at 10pm, arriving at Lao Cai station the next morning at 6–7am. Sapa hotels will organise transfers for the 39-km (24-mile) drive from Lao Cai to Sapa.

A comfortable budget-priced option is the **Auberge Dang Trung Hotel** (tel: 020-871 243; e-mail: sapanow@yahoo.com); book one of the top-floor rooms which have magnificent views of the 'Tonkinese Alps'. Inquire about package deals with transfers and tours. Alternatively, if money is no object, book a package with the more upmarket **Victoria Sapa Hotel** (tel: 020-871

Above: terraced hill slopes of Sa Pa

522; www.victoriahotels-asia.com), which transfers its guests on board its luxurious **Victoria Express Train** – departing Hanoi four times weekly.

An Unexplored Paradise

Sa Pa, located over 1,000m (3,280ft) and a former French hill station has a special charm, bustling with montagnards (*see page 16*) and set against breathtaking mountains. Sa Pa was a small Hmong tribal village until 1918 when a group of Jesuits established a now-defunct order there. They were swiftly followed by the French colonialists who built a 600-house hill station to escape the heat of Hanoi, half of which was destroyed during the First Indochina War.

The main reason to come to Sapa is the opportunity to trek through ethnic minority villages, staying overnight in local stilt houses – especially since government restrictions have been lifted. Several outlying villages – **Cat Cat**, **Ta Van**, **Sin Chai**, **Lao Chai** and **Ta Phin** – make pleasant, relatively easy treks. However, as these villages are becoming increasingly commercialised, many operators are now venturing further afield, hiking to more remote mountain villages and scenery. Try and trek with a local guide, as they understand the local dialects, etiquette and customs better and are able to explain a good deal more. Recommended local tour operators include **Topas Adventure Vietnam** (11 Cau May Street, tel: 020-871331; Hanoi branch, tel: 04-928 3637; www.topas-adventure-vietnam.com) and the aforementioned Auberge Dang Trung.

There are two main tribes inhabiting this area, Hmong or Meo, and Red Zao. The Zao are striking for their elaborate headdress but they are also the shyest and do not like being photographed. The Hmong can be quite pushy. You may find yourself swamped by sales-happy Hmong, all eagerly dressing you with the different garments they have for sale while tittering '*jolie, jolie*' (pretty, pretty in French) in a high-pitched chorus.

Sapa used to be sold on the pretext of a Saturday night '**Love Market**', where young minorities coyly met potential suitors in the town centre. However, this form of voyeuristic tourism has been stopped, and the tradition has moved to a more secluded area. The weekend central **Sapa Market** is worth investigating, and there are some fascinating, remote weekly ethnic minority markets, several hours from Sapa, which offer more traditional market life. **Can Cau** (Saturday), **Coc Ly** (Tuesday) and **Muong Hom** (Sunday), all near the Chinese border, are highly recommended. Arrange a tour or hire a jeep (roughly US$50–60) with a reputable local operator.

If you are fit and healthy, consider making the ascent to **Mount Fansipan**, at 3,143m (10, 251ft) and the highest mountain in Vietnam. Fansipan is only about 10km (6 miles) from Sa Pa but the climb is difficult – warm clothes, good boots and camping equipment are essential as are the services of a trekking agency.

Right: minority hilltribes near Sa Pa

Leisure Activities

SHOPPING

Almost everything in Vietnam is for sale. From classic Citroens to postcards clutched in children's hands you will be quoted a price instantly if you show the slightest trace of an interest. In the first few years after *doi moi* and comparative economic relaxation, this was often a nuisance, as street vendors and touts were very persistent indeed by relaxed Southeast Asian standards. More recently, however, the authorities seem to have realised the negative impact such insistence can have on tourism, and harassment of visitors by street vendors is diminishing – though it can still be a trial.

While the first price you hear will always be too high, the Vietnamese appreciate a good haggler. If you demand the 'correct' price they will give it to you happily, and respect you all the more. The difficulty is finding out what the 'correct' price is. Vietnamese have a low opinion of people who pay too much for things and will always be curious about how much you paid for an item. Admitting that you paid 50 cents over the top can make you an object of ridicule, but getting a bargain raises your street credibility by leaps and bounds. On the other hand, there is nothing more demeaning than watching a traveller arguing with a dirt-poor *cyclo* driver over the equivalent of what amounts to five American cents.

Prices are generally low in Vietnam. There are exceptions, such as new vehicles and imported alcohol, but by and large, prices are less than you expect. If air-conditioned and sanitized shopping malls are anathema to you then Vietnam is the place to be. The air is always thick with different smells and the sounds of haggling. Shops selling the same items cluster together in one street and markets have stall after stall specializing in similar goods. You get a better price by enquiring at each stall and allowing the price to fall as the vendors undercut one another. Remember always to smile and be polite – you will get a better price and retain your dignity, while at the same time making the vendors around you happy, even if they don't make a sale.

Vietnamese shop for groceries early in the morning. Market shopping tends to be more relaxed in the afternoons when the traders have cooled off a little. In the cities, shopping hours are usually 7.30–11.30am and 1.30–4.30pm, but increasingly, more shops stay open until 6.30pm or later.

Travellers cheques and credit cards are making an appearance in Vietnam, but mainly for hotel bills and cash transfers. You will certainly have to use cash to pay for goods and services, and in most cases the local currency, dong.

Ho Chi Minh City

This city is a treasure trove for shoppers. A mixed bag of goods, like traditional basket-ware, computers, SLR cameras, imported clothes and war paraphernalia are available

Left: a flower vendor at Hue's market
Right: baskets and puppets for sale

in the city centre or in Cholon. Ask your hotel reception for places where more unusual items can be found.

Dong Khoi Street and the streets immediately off it have the best souvenir shops. You will find silks, lacquerware and embroideries in abundance, and if you're lucky, more unusual buys like intricately-carved opium pipes. Tailors like **Khaisilk** at No 107 and **Song** at No 41 are good and many speak English, so take the opportunity to have some clothes made for a fraction of the cost in Europe and US. The more expensive tailors carry wool and heavier fabrics for jackets and suits.

In the **Thieves Market** between Nguyen Hue and Ho Tung Mao streets you will find cheap electronic goods, DVDs and CDs. If you have time on your hands you can have bootleg CDs made to order.

Ben Thanh, at the end of Le Loi Street, is the main city market, equipped with everything from towels and wigs to cosmetics and vegetables. Look out for shady straw hats to keep the sun out and round fabric ones with pigtails sewn in for children. Be warned that this area is notorious for pickpockets and you should carry your bag or purse in front of you.

The roads around **Binh Tay** market in Cholon have Buddhist gongs and drums

cheaper than in Hue. You can buy incense in large spirals or long sticks decorated with flowers. If you are a keen photographer, a 6am trip to Cholon will reward you with huge numbers of livestock congregating in the markets. Ducks, chickens, pigs and a dazzling array of vegetables, flowers and other produce fill the market each morning.

Hanoi

The **Old Quarter** – bordered by the railway line and the north side of Hoan Kiem Lake – is filled with little boutiques and stalls overflowing with an astonishing array of goods. Cheap Chinese electronic products (probably smuggled in), food, baskets, clothes, Chinese herbal medicine; the list is endless. **Dong Xuan Market**, the main covered market in Hanoi, was rebuilt after being damaged by fire, and is once again open for business. The streets leading to it however are still packed, so browse around and take your pick.

Buy silk, which is fractionally cheaper in Hanoi than Ho Chi Minh City, from shops in **Hang Gai Street**. Exquisite silk clothes and accessories from **Khaisilk** at No 96 are recommended. Also try **Kenly Silk** at No 108. **Le Vent**, 115 Hang Gai Street, specialises in modern takes on traditional designs in sheer organza while **Cocoon**, 30 Nha Chung Street, sells taffeta silk with intricate embroidery.

Embroidery – a timeless Vietnamese craft– is another Hanoi speciality. Many shops – especially on Hang Gai Street – sell embroidery and drawn threadwork, although quality varies. **Tan My**, at 66 and 109 Hang Gai Street are reputable outlets selling hand-embroidered work with traditional designs on natural fabrics.

Lacquerware is another excellent buy in Hanoi. Countless shops sell lacquerware boxes, bowls, photograph albums, vases and trays, but not all of them made in the traditional method. Mass-produced, synthetic lacquer products have swamped the market, which can't compare with traditional lacquerware in both durability and charm. Look

Left: jumping catfish

out for more contemporary lacquerware, hand-made but with a more modern style, sometimes with Japanese-influenced shapes and a matt finish. **Minh Tam**, 2 Hang Bong Street, specialises in black and white eggshell lacquerware.

Particularly around **Nha Tho Street**, near St Joseph's Cathedral, innovative home decor and interior design shops combine Asian flair with contemporary Western designs, using traditional local materials such as wood, silk, buffalo horn, lacquer and bamboo. Quality stores include **Mosaique**, No 22 and Italian-run **LaCasa**, No 12, on Nha Tho Street and **Dome**, 71 Hang Trong Street (also 10 Yen The Street).

Several shops sell antiques and objets d'art, but it's difficult telling the genuine from reproductions. Recommended are **Nguyen Freres**, 3 Phan Chu Trinh and 9 Dinh Tien Hoang streets and **Red Door Deco**, 15 Nha Tho Street. **Nha San Duc**, the house on stilts (*see page 65*) has a selection of 'distressed' Buddhas and statues, and other artefacts aged to look antique. Au Co Street (the extension of Nghi Tam) in the north of the city also has numerous antiques shops.

Contemporary Vietnamese art has undergone rapid change in the last decade, especially in Hanoi, which is regarded as Vietnam's artistic centre. With international recognition for Vietnamese art, there has been an explosion of art galleries in Hanoi. Recommended dealers include **Apricot Gallery** at 40B, **Mai Gallery** at 183 and **Salon Natasha** at 30 – all along Hang Bong Street. Also reputable are **Art Vietnam Gallery** at 30 Hang Than and **Green Palm Gallery** at 110 Hang Gai.

Hue

Watch out for the unique 'poem hats' which make excellent and inexpensive souvenirs. In Hue the characteristic *non la* conical hats worn by Vietnamese women everywhere are particularly fine and some may be held up to the light to reveal traditional Viet scenes in silhouette. Also, rice paper and silk paintings are worthwhile buys.

Hoi An

Hoi An is primarily famous for its many boutiques and tailors who can sew up an outfit in hours. Allow time for alterations. **A Dong Silk** at 40 Le Loi Street or **Thu Thuy** at 60 Le Loi Street are recommended.

Da Lat

The **Central Market** in Da Lat has a cornucopia of souvenirs. The three-storey structure (food on the ground floor, souvenirs and clothes on the top two levels) dates from 1958 and is found at the end of Nguyen Thi Minh Khai and Le Dai Hanh streets. In the market square and carried aloft on the backs of street vendors you will find material and basketware made by ethnic minorities and delightfully fragrant dried teas.

Nha Trang

The **Dam Market** is a good one-stop shop for tourist souvenirs. Jewellery and decorations made from shell are best at **Cau Da Port**. Tortoiseshell glasses and necklaces are really made from turtle shell, and there seems to be no regulation about their use. Thankfully, the ivory-like material used in the jewellery is fish bone.

Above: Nha San's 'distressed' Buddha

EATING OUT

If you haven't tried Vietnamese cuisine you are in for a treat. Food in Vietnam is a constant surprise: delicate, cheap and available in an endless string of combinations. The most genuine (and some of the best) Vietnamese food is sampled on the street, where stallkeepers specialize in just one dish and serve the freshest food.

Keep a sharp lookout for handwritten signs over steaming cauldrons surrounded by toy-sized chairs. *Com* or rice is the staple, topped with meat, fish and vegetables, and accompanied by *nuoc mam* (fish sauce) or *nuoc tuong* (soya sauce). *Pho* (noodles) is the most common street food and makes a tasty snack at any time of the day. Hot soup is poured over noodles, spices and herbs are added and topped with either beef (*bo*) or chicken (*ga*). Other snacks to look out for are *bun* and *banh hoi*, noodles served with meat and fish sauce, *banh cuon*, a thin pancake rolled and chopped into portions, and *banh beo*, fat Chinese-style dumplings filled with pork and egg.

Other popular Vietnamese dishes include *cha gio* (known as *nem Saigon* in the north): small 'spring rolls' of minced pork, prawn, crabmeat, fragrant mushrooms and vegetables wrapped in thin rice paper and then deep fried. *Cha gio* is rolled in a lettuce leaf with fresh mint and other herbs, then dipped in a sweet sauce. *Chao tom* is a northern delicacy: finely minced shrimp baked on a stick of sugar cane, then eaten with lettuce, cucumber, coriander (cilantro) and mint, and dipped in fish sauce. Another dish eaten in a similar fashion is *cuon diep*, or shrimp, noodles, mint, coriander and pork wrapped in lettuce leaves. Hue, a city associated with Buddhism, is famous for its vegetarian cuisine and for its *banh khoai*, or 'Hue pancake'. A batter of rice flour and corn is fried with egg to make a pancake, then wrapped around pork or shrimp, onion, bean sprouts and mushrooms. Another Hue speciality is *bun bo*, or fried beef and noodles served with coriander, onion, garlic, cucumber, chilli peppers and tomato paste.

The last few years have seen an explosion of bistro-style restaurants in Hanoi and Ho Chi Minh City. Viet Kieu (overseas Vietnamese) and foreign-Vietnamese partnerships (often husband-and-wife teams) have been opening a rash of new restaurants, catering mainly to foreign tastes. New establishments are mushrooming all the time, so there may be discrepancies between the ones described here and what you find.

The array of fruits available is amazing. They include many lush tropical fruits such as mango, custard apple, sapodilla, durian, pineapple, star fruit, and rambutan. Dalat strawberries are sold in the spring throughout the country as the road and rail network now allows the fast transport of delicate fruits and vegetables. Look out also for dragon fruit, a magenta-coloured fruit whose white flesh is speckled with black seeds. Found all over the country, with the exception of Hanoi, are *sinh to* stalls, recognizable by their glass cases displaying a variety of fruits and vegetables. Point to a selection of fruit and you will receive a thick shake, with or without sugar (*duong*).

On a hot day, the best non-alcoholic drink is *nuoc chanh da* or *soda chanh*, lemon juice with ice or soda. Orange juice comes pre-sugared, as does coffee. Vietnamese coffee is very strong and comes iced (*co da*) or hot (*nong*). Milk (*sua*) is usually condensed unless you are in a place that often serves foreigners. Bottled fresh water, canned and bottled soft drinks and a wide range of canned beers are available throughout the country. French and Australian wines are increasingly popular, especially at French restaurants. Local rice liquors are cheap but potent.

Beware of restaurants with no prices on the menu. It is acceptable to ask first. It is best to arrive in Vietnamese restaurants (especially the smaller ones) by noon for lunch and 7.30pm for dinner as food can run out early. The approximate cost of a meal for two people without alcohol is as follows:

$$$ = over US$20
$$ = US$10–20
$ = less than US$10

Ho Chi Minh City

Asian Reflections
Caravelle Hotel
19 Lam Son Square, District 1
Tel: 08-823 4999
Cutting-edge Asian fusion cuisine plated Western-style. Stylish upmarket atmosphere and excellent service. $$$

Bo Tung Xeo Restaurant
31 Ly Tu Truong
Tel: 08-825 1330
Huge Vietnamese grilled beef restaurant. The beef is the big draw, but for the daring, there are deep fried scorpions and 'jumping prawns'. Popular and quite rightly so. $

Lemon Grass
4 Nguyen Thiep, District 1
Tel: 08-822 0496
A consistent favourite for delicious and inventive Vietnamese food. $$

Nam Phan
64 Le Thanh Ton Street, District 1
Tel: 08-829 2757
A lovely high-end Vietnamese eatery housed in a restored old villa decorated with silks and antiques. Run by the owner of Khaisilk. $$$

Pho Hoa
260C Pasteur Street, District 3
This café-style eatery is found just where the street divides at the top end. Succulent chicken breast tops a flavoursome broth with crisp shallots and *pho* (noodles). $

Pomodoro
79 Hai Ba Trung, District 1
Tel: 08-823 8957
The best in Italian dining at this friendly place with wood-fired oven pizzas, great lasagne and daily specials. The owner makes his own wonderful Grappa liquer. $$

Quan An Ngon
138 Nam Ky Khoi Nghia
Tel: 08-829 9449
Fantastic recreation of a street stall eatery with style. Excellent traditional Vietnamese standards and all very reasonably priced. A popular lunchtime spot. $

Skewers
8A/1/D2 Thai Van Lung Street, District 1
Tel: 08-829 2216
Mediterranean restaurant, café and bar serving a wide range of dishes, including skew-

Left: piquant and mildly spicy best describes Vietnamese cuisine
Above: 'Banh Xeo' pancake vendor

ered meat, hence the name. Good wine list, friendly owner and a relaxed setting. $$

Song Ngu Seafood Restaurant
70–72 Suong Nguyet Anh Street, District 1
Tel: 08-832 5017
Come here for some of the best and freshest seafood dining in the city: crabs in tamarind sauce, crispy squid with onion and herbs, and 'drunken' prawns marinaded in wine are just some of the specials here.

Tan Nam
60–62 Dong Du, District 1
Tel: 08-829 8634
Delicious Vietnamese fare in a French colonial setting just off Dong Khoi Street. Cosy candle-lit atmosphere. $$

The Camargue
16 Cao Ba Quat
Tel: 08-824 3148
A villa with an open terrace and gardens is the setting for one of the prettiest French restaurant in town. Good for lunch, with a well-stocked bar and pool tables. $$$

Hanoi

Brother's Café
26 Nguyen Thai Hoc Street
Tel: 04-733 3866

Charming Vietnamese restaurant set in a colonial villa and serving authentic dishes buffet-style. Both indoor and outdoor seating available. Excellent value for money. $$

Bun Cha
20 Ta Hien Street, 1 Hanh Manh
Fantastic lunch dish of noodles and grilled pork served all over Hanoi. These places serve the best versions in town. $

Cay Cau
De Syloia Hotel, 17A Tran Hung Dao
Tel: 04-933 1010
Excellent Vietnamese food that is popular among people in the know. The pomelo salad, crabs in tamarind and pork-stuffed egg plant are all highly recommended. $$

Le Beaulieu
Sofitel Metropole, 15 Ngo Quyen
Tel: 04-826 6919
Dine here if only to soak in the French colonial atmosphere of this beautiful restaurant. Its lavish Sunday brunch is an institution among Hanoi's well-heeled. $$$

Luna d'Autunno
11B Dien Bien Phu Street
Tel: 04-823 7338
This restaurant serves Hanoi's best pizza and pasta dishes. It has a cosy outdoor seating area and is run by Italians, so expect friendly services. $$$

Restaurant Bobby Chinn
1 Ba Trieu Street
Tel: 04-934 8577
Fusion Californian-Asian cuisine using organic produce and completed by stunning surroundings of silk drapes and cushions, candles and contemporary art. Attracts a chi chi crowd. Excellent wine list. $$$

Spices Garden
Sofitel Metropole, 15 Ngo Quyen Street
Tel: 04-826 6919
A fabulous hybrid of North Vietnamese cuisine with creative French influences and

Left: street vendor whipping up delicious Vietnamese food

flavours. Lunchtime 'mock' Hanoi street food stalls provide a sanitised introduction to local cuisine. $$

The Vine
1A Xuan Dieu, West Lake
Tel: 04-719 8000
The mainly Western menu in this cosy and intimate place has some nice Asian accents: try Nok's Thai spaghetti and the wood-fired Hanoi pizza. Excellent range of wines. $$

Phu Quoc

Apple Garden (Vuon Tau)
5km south of Duong Dong
Tel: 077-847 228
This garden restaurant, set in the middle of a field, serves fried fish on rice paper. $

Mai House
Long Beach (250m south of Tropicana)
Tel: 077-847 003
French Vietnamese food in an idyllic setting. $$

Dalat

Café de la Poste
12 Tran Phu
Tel: 063-825 777
This triangular building across from the Cathedral has styled itself as a café of the 1950s, when Dalat was popular with the elite from Saigon. $$$

Nha Trang

Cho Dem
On the beach across from 98 Tran Phu
This night food market has stalls from the best family-owned restaurants in the city. Most of these serve their own seafood specialities. A good way of experiencing the street food of Vietnam. Open 6 to 11pm. $

Lac Canh Restaurant
11 Hang Ca
Tel: 058-828 129
Some of the best seafood in this port city grilled at your table. Get there early as this place fills up quickly. $

Danang

Tu Do Restaurant
172 Tran Phu Street
Tel: 0511-821 869
Vietnamese food, with a sprinkling of dishes from other cuisines in a garden setting. $$

Hoi An

Café des Amis
52 Bach Dang
Tel: 0510-861 616
Hoi An's original seafood restaurant is still going strong after many a year at the top of the favourites list of many travellers. $$

Cargo Club Restaurant
107–9 Nguyen Thai Hoc Street
Tel: 0510-910 489
Charming French-owned place with excellent cakes and sandwiches. At night Vietnamese and Western fare are served. $$

Hue

Club Garden
8 Vo Thi Sau
Tel: 054-826 327
Dine in a small garden or at the air-conditioned dining room; the speciality is Hue food. $$

Ong Tao
5 Pham Ngu Lao
Tel: 054-821 732
Delicious Hue-style food in this newly relocated restaurant. $$

Right: hands off my pizza

NIGHTLIFE

The polarity between rural and urban lifestyles in Vietnam is nowhere more glaringly obvious than when it comes to nightlife. In a country where people habitually rise at 4.30am, it is little surprise that a drink at 9.30pm may be construed as a late night out. In the big cities, where incomes are rising and foreign influences felt, this attitude has all but disappeared. Bright lights come on, CD players are spun and cocktails served in increasing quantities. The night is coming to life.

At weekends, youth culture in Ho Chi Minh City and Hanoi parades itself in glorious technicolour. Cruising down Ho Chi Minh's fashionable Dong Khoi Street or around Hanoi's Hoan Kiem Lake on a motorcycle and enjoying the more liberal atmosphere is now de rigueur for the city's outgoing youth.

Although *bia hoi* establishments exist in other large cities, they are most popular in Hanoi. These small, downmarket bars cater exclusively to men – though there would be no objections to a Western woman sitting down for a drink – serving 'fresh beer' without preservatives at amazingly low prices. Vietnamese high society is scarcely likely to patronise these bars, but ordinary Vietnamese workers often stop by for a glass on the way home. They can be good places to meet the locals, but usually run out of beer early and close by 8 or 9pm.

Cafés everywhere stay open reasonably late and are filled with couples chatting or just listening to music. Vietnamese generally tend not to drink coffee late at night, and you will probably be offered tea.

Karaoke bars are extremely popular with the Vietnamese. If you're lucky enough to wrangle an invitation to somebody's home karaoke get-together, you will get a very different insight into the Vietnamese side of this addictive diversion.

Old-fashioned dances like the waltz and mambo are alive and kicking at traditional dance halls. But, there are also modern discos where ravers bop to the latest house music.

Ho Chi Minh City

Pounding rock can be heard once again in the backstreets of Ho Chi Minh City's District 1. From the state-of-the-art Q Bar to smoke-filled *bia hoi*, you will find every type of drinking establishment here.

Apocalypse Now
2C Thi Sach Street, District 1
Tel: 08-824 1463
The best known bar in town has become *the* best bar in town. Loud music attracts avid party-goers. Ad lib dancing after midnight.

Aquarium Café Sango
102 Nam Ky Khoi Nghia, District 1
Tel: 08-827 5593
Cool blue interior, flooded with hip house beats on Fridays and Saturdays. More

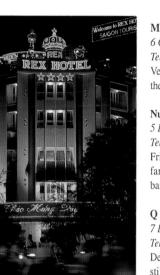

Shibuya than Saigon with nine aquariums filled with moray eels and angler fish.

Café Latin
25 Dong Du Street, District 1
Tel: 08-226 363
Laid back tapas bar and café, with big screen TV. Popular with local sports fans.

Catwalk International Tourist Club
76 Le Lai, District 1
Tel: 08-824 3760
This disco is very popular with Korean and Japanese tourists. There are several karaoke rooms, a large dance floor and many very glamorous hostesses.

Gecko Bar
74/1A Hai Ba Trung, District 1
Tel: 08-824 2754
Popular expat haunt offering billiards, darts, satellite TV, and good food and music.

Hoa Vien Brauhaus
28B Mac Dinh Chi, District 1
Tel: 08-825 8605
Authentic Bavarian beerhall and micro-brewery serving the best beer in Vietnam. Also dishes up hearty European fare including deep fried cheese and some Vietnamese staples.

Left: revving up the night
Above: Rex Hotel's rooftop bar is tops

Maya Bar
6 Cao Ba Quat, District 1
Tel: 08-829 5180
Very stylish, trendy joint with free drinks for the fairer sex on 'Ladies Night' (Wednesday).

Number 5 Bar
5 Ly Tu Trong Street, District 1
Tel: 08-825 6300
Friendly service and popular with football fans. Pool table, draught beer and a basic bar snack menu.

Q Bar
7 Lam Son Square, District 1
Tel: 08-823 5424
Despite competition from other bars, this is still one of the coolest places for the hip to be seen. Has an extensive selection of drinks and plays good jazz music.

Saigon Saigon Bar
Caravelle Hotel, 19 Lam Son Square, District 1
Tel: 08-823 4999
Has become a staple drinking haven because of the view. This pleasant place offers bar food, drinks, decent cocktails and live music from the in-house band.

Tropical Rainforest
5-15 Ho Huan Nghiep, District 1
Tel: 08-825 7783
Themed to look like the Amazon (well, nearly). Very popular among young Vietnamese.

Underground
Lucky Plaza Basement, 69 Dong Khoi, District 1
Tel: 08-829 9079
One of the few live music venues opened till late on weekends. Also serves great burgers, nachos, Middle Eastern food and salads.

Vasco's Bar
16 Cao Ba Quat, District 1
Tel: 08-824 3148
Outdoor/indoor bar and disco. Live bands

every Friday. This is a very popular expatriate hangout which doesn't start filling up until 11pm.

Hanoi

After years of complaints from tourists that it is impossible to have a late night in Hanoi, the city has fought back with a slew of new bars and discos. You will find tipples and atmospheres to suit all tastes. If not, there is always the *bia hoi* for drinking beer.

Bobby Chinn
1 Ba Trieu
Tel: 04-934 8578
Atmospheric bar and restaurant run by the ebullient chef, Bobby. Very popular with foreign residents.

Funky Monkey Bar
15B Hang Hanh
Tel: 04-928 6113
Narrow bar, popular with a younger crowd with boisterous DJs and pool room.

Jazz Club
31 Luong Van Can
Tel: 04-828 7890
Popular jazz club in the Old Quarter. Other type of bands play too including some young Vietnamese rock bands.

New Century
10 Trang Thi
Tel: 04-928 5285
The most favoured nightspot for young and affluent Vietnamese. Huge dance floor, lightshow, go-go dancers and DJs.

R & R Tavern
47 Lo Su
Tel: 04-934 4109
Long-established bar, run by a laid-back American. Step back in time and listen to the great music of the 60s, of which this place boasts an impressive CD collection. Bar food includes a selection of Tex Mex dishes. Very popular with resident expats.

Spotted Cow
23C Hai Ba Trung
Tel: 04-824 1028
Very popular expat drinking den with a dart board and pool table.

The Terrace Bar
Press Club, 59A Ly Thai To
Tel: 04-934 0888
Has a wide selection of drinks and live music. Very popular with expats and locals. 'Happy Hour' with drinks at discounted prices on Friday nights is especially popular.

The Wave Bar & Club
Sofitel Plaza Hanoi, 1 Thanh Nien
Tel: 04-823 8888
Party lovers will enjoy the loud music, large dance floor and big screen video at this popular weekend night spot on the edge of Ho Tay (West Lake).

Above: late-night pool at a Hanoi bar

CALENDAR OF EVENTS

Celebrations in Vietnam fall between one of two camps: new and Communist, or traditional and according to the lunar calendar; the latter with dates that vary every year.

January – February

Tet (1st day of the lunar year), a four-day official holiday – the most important of Vietnamese festivals – is celebrated with a bang. According to legend, the gods of the house fly up to heaven one week before the Lunar New Year to report on how well behaved the family has been. When the gods return on the eve of the new lunar year, they are welcomed with firecrackers and parties. This racket was muffled in 1995 when the government banned the use of fireworks throughout the country.

In the week before the Lunar New Year, roads, trains and planes become clogged with overseas Vietnamese rushing home for the festivities. Hotels are also fully booked during this period.

Dong Ky Fire Cracker Festival (4th day of the 1st lunar month) in Ha Bac and Ha Son Binh provinces is the loudest and largest, although the festivities are taped noises today because firecrackers are banned.

Elephant Race Day (10th day of the 1st lunar month) is a typical ethnic festival in the Central Highlands.

Hoi Lim Festival (13th day of the 1st lunar month) takes place in Ha Bac province. Here, girls and boys sing courtship songs to one another.

Hai Ba Trung (6th day of the 2nd lunar month). In Hanoi, at Hai Ba Trung Temple, this festival honours the heroic resistance of the Trung sisters against the Chinese.

March – April

Perfume Pagoda Festival (2nd day of the 2nd lunar month). Thousands descend on the grottoes and shrines in this holy area in Ha Son Binh province southwest of Hanoi.

Liberation Day (30 April) marking the liberation of Saigon in 1975 is celebrated with Labour Day (1 May) as a double festival.

Right: Dong Ky's fire cracker of a festival

May – June

Tet Duan Ngo (5th day of the 5th lunar month). The summer solstice is celebrated to ensure good health and well-being.

Ho Chi Minh's Birthday (19 May). Speeches, wreath-laying at shrines and performances in theatres around the country.

July – August

Trang Nguyen (14th day of the 7th lunar month). Day of Lost Souls. Tombs are cleansed and offerings made to spirits.

September – October

National Day (2 September). A national holiday commemorating the Declaration of Independence in 1945, which founded the Democratic Republic of Vietnam.

Mid-Autumn Festival (15th day of the 8th lunar month). Children parade around with candle-illuminated lanterns, and delicious pastry-covered 'mooncakes' with sweet lotus seed or red bean paste are eaten.

Whale Festival (16th day of the 8th lunar month). Crowds gather to make offerings to whales at Vung Tau, where the great sea creatures are venerated.

December

Christmas (25 December). Celebrated by Christians who go to church for the midnight mass and enjoy much merry-making on the streets after.

Practical Information

GETTING THERE

By Air
Cathay Pacific, Air France, Qantas, Singapore Airlines, Eva Air, Malaysia Airlines, Thai Airways, KLM, British Airways and Lufthansa fly to Vietnam together with the national carrier, Vietnam Airlines. Ho Chi Minh City is the main gateway, with fewer international flights going to Hanoi. It is also possible to fly direct to Danang from Bangkok, Hongkong and Singapore.

Ho Chi Minh City's **Tan Son Nhat Airport** is 7km (4¼ miles) from downtown and is a 15-minute ride by metered airport taxi. In Hanoi, **Noi Bai Airport** is located 35km (21 miles) away from the city centre. Travel time is 45 to 60 minutes by taxi.

By Rail
It is possible to enter Vietnam from southern China by train but you have to change trains and walk across the border at Lao Cai.

By Road
You can access Vietnam by road from China, Cambodia and Laos. Since 1993 it has been possible to drive from Bangkok to Ho Chi Minh City via Phnom Penh, although most roads in Cambodia are quite appalling. Make sure that you have the correct entry/exit visa requirements before approaching customs.

By Sea
Expensive cruise ships stop by Vietnam, usually staying for only a few days as part of a Southeast Asian tour. Merchant ships enter via the ports of Ho Chi Minh City, Haiphong, Vung Tau and Danang. You might, with difficulty, be able to organise a private yacht landing here. Check with a Vietnamese embassy for the proper documentation.

Left: a *cyclo* driver taking shelter
Right: train routes link cities in Vietnam

TRAVEL ESSENTIALS

When to Visit
The sun is always shining somewhere in Vietnam. The country stretches 1,650km (1,000 miles) from top to toe, and you should be prepared for both heat and rain. Ho Chi Minh City is fairly hot (21–36°C/70–97°F) all year round, with the rainy season stretching from May to November. It can rain for 20–30 minutes each time, usually in the afternoons and early evenings. Hanoi is generally cooler and goes through greater extremes (8–33°C/46–91°F). Summers from May to September are hot and humid with the most rainfall during this period. Winter is generally dry and chilly although February and March sees lingering grey and drizzly days. Central Vietnam from Danang to Nha Trang has its own weather patterns: the dry season is from January to September, with the most rainfall from October to mid-January.

Tet, the national festival, is a moveable two-week celebration (depending on the lunar calendar) when a riot of merrymaking renders it virtually impossible to organise anything in Vietnam (see page 87).

Visas and Passports
It used to be incredibly difficult for independent travellers to gain entry to Vietnam in

the past. Today, it is fairly straightforward to get a visa. Ask the travel agent from whom you buy your air ticket to arrange it for you. The cost of a one-month single-entry visa is from US$30. There will probably be a commission charge on top of the visa processing fee paid to the visa office of the Vietnamese embassy or consulate. Individual travellers may also apply for a visa directly with the Vietnamese embassy or consulate in their home country but this might prove tedious.

For a list of foreign missions overseas, check the **Vietnamese Ministry of Foreign Affairs** website at www.mofa.gov.vn.

Visas may be extended whilst in Vietnam; check with a local travel agency for details.

Customs

Be forewarned that Vietnamese customs officers can be difficult to deal with, so make sure you have all your papers in order before you join the customs queue. When you arrive you will need to fill in the requisite customs declaration forms and a landing card, which you must keep and produce when leaving the country. Video tapes, DVDs, CDs, cameras, industrial equipment and electronic gadgets can all fall under heavy scrutiny.

Police Registration

Internal travel permits are no longer required for visiting major tourist areas in Vietnam but hotels and guesthouses outside of Hanoi and Ho Chi Minh City may ask for your passport for police registration. The staff will return it to you the next morning. In Hanoi

or Ho Chi Minh City, hotels may only require your landing card, from which they will fill in details in a book and then return it. In other places, the staff may insist on holding your passport for your entire stay.

Note that procedures and policies change constantly and often without warning. If you must turn over your passport, make sure that the correct one – and the landing card – are returned to you.

Vaccinations

No vaccinations are mandatory but local medical authorities recommend protection against polio, diphtheria, typhoid, tetanus, hepatitis A and B, and Japanese encephalitis. For travellers spending much time in the countryside, anti-malaria pills are recommended and you should take precautions with repellents and mosquito nets.

Clothing

Vietnam is a very relaxed country when it comes to attire. There are virtually no religious dictates, although monks prefer people not to wear singlets and shorts when visiting holy sites. Vietnamese admire neatness and cleanliness above sartorial finesse and you will be treated with more respect if you take pains to dress accordingly.

Loose cotton clothes are recommended, and waterproof footwear for the rainy season. It is easiest to wear slip-off shoes as you will have to remove them when you visit houses and temples. A foldable umbrella is useful if you are caught in showers.

Time

Vietnam is 7 hours ahead of Greenwich Mean Time (GMT).

Electricity

Electricity in Ho Chi Minh City is rated at either 220 or 110 volts, with the former starting to be the norm in most cities these days. The most common power points are two-pin; both round and flat prongs are equally common. It is best to bring a multi-prong travel adapter with you.

Above: Vietnamese children

GETTING ACQUAINTED

Geography

Set at the eastern edge of Indochina, Vietnam's 3,260-km (2,037-mile) coastline borders the South China Sea. The S-shaped country features two river deltas, the Mekong in the south and Red River in the north. About 70 percent of the Vietnamese live in these two alluvial plains, cultivating rice. The Central Highlands create a high divide between the north and south, and the Northern Highlands shield Hanoi from China and Laos. Major highways tend to run from north to south and rivers from west to east.

Government & Administration

Vietnam is a Communist country governed by a single party system run by the Quoc Hoi (National Assembly), elected once every five years. The Quoc Hoi meets for short sessions twice annually. When it is not in session, a Council of State issues ordinances for ultimate approval by the Quoc Hoi. The President, Prime Minister and Cabinet are appointed by the Quoc Hoi.

The republic is divided into 53 administrative areas: three cities – Hanoi, Ho Chi Minh City and Hai Phong – and 64 provinces. Provincial officials maintain some level of independence in implementing state policy.

Religion

Mahayana Buddhism is the main religion although ancestor worship is still widely practised. You will find altars in many houses, with offerings and photographs of parents and grandparents. Confucian philosophy has influenced morals, and family ties are strong. Familial loyalty and obedience are central to the Vietnamese social structure. The Taoist idea of balance and harmony has also influenced the Vietnamese world view.

Nearly 10 percent of the population are Catholic. There is a substantial Theravada Buddhist minority among the ethnic Khmers of the Mekong Delta, and there are small Muslim communities of South Asian origin in Hanoi and Ho Chi Minh City.

Population

Some 87 percent are of Vietnam's 83.5 million people are Kinh or Vietnamese (descendants of the Lac people), 2 percent ethnic Chinese or Hoa, and the rest Khmers, Chams and montagnards (mountain people).

How Not To Offend

Always be polite, never lose your temper and expect things to take longer than you expect. The idea of saving 'face' is an important Vietnamese concept for the visitor to grasp. Avoid placing a Vietnamese in a position where he or she has to admit to being wrong.

MONEY MATTERS

Currency

The Vietnamese dong (pronounced *dom*) is the national currency. As the dong is not a convertible currency, you cannot legally bring in or take out dong as a foreigner. Although most transactions are carried out in dong, US dollars are readily acceptable. US$1 is roughly equivalent to about 15,800 dong at time of press, but the currency is subject to fluctuation. Notes are in denominations of 100, 200, 500, 1,000, 2,000, 5,000, 10,000, 20,000, 50,000 and 100,000, 500,000, and coins are in denominations of 5,000, 2,000, 1,000, 500 and 200 dong.

Credit Cards & Travellers' Cheques

Visa, Amex, JCB, Diners Club and Master-Card are accepted at some banks and most large hotels. An increasing number of shops and restaurants now accept major credit cards. Travellers' cheques, preferably in US dollars, can be easily cashed at banks, hotels and some travel agents.

Money-changers

Street money-changers have all but disappeared. Don't deal with them as they have a bad reputation for cheating. Branches of the Vietcombank, large hotels and most gold shops will change money for you at the correct exchange rate. Although most vendors

the country. There are flights connecting Ho Chi Minh City and Hanoi and between these cities and hubs such as Da Lat, Nha Trang, Danang, Hue and other major cities, and also some other remote spots.

Vietnam Airlines' Ho Chi Minh City office is at 116 Nguyen Hue, District 1 (tel: 08-832 0320); the Hanoi office is located at 1 Quang Trung Street (tel: 04-832 0320). Flights are relatively expensive.

Pacific Airlines serves domestic customers on many of the same routes (www. pacificairlines.com.vn) and **VASCO Airlines** (114B Bach Dang, HCMC tel: 08-844 5999) has flights to Ca Mau in the far south and Con Dao Island.

Trains

The Reunification Express, operated by **Vietnam Railways** (www.vr.com.vn), travels along the north-south axis of the country, linking Ho Chi Minh City with Hanoi and making stops at many towns along the way. The journey can take up to 30–41 hours and is popular with die-hard train aficionados. Book seats a few days before and pay a little bit more for the air-conditioned bottom sleeper. This allows you to place your luggage under your bunk while you sleep. There have been cases of burglaries on board so bring a padlock and chain to secure your luggage to some unmovable part of the train. Food and drinks are available on the trains, and hawkers clamber on at the stops to sell snacks.

In Ho Chi Minh City, the train station is at 1 Nguyen Thong Street, tel: 08-823 0105. In Hanoi, go to 120 Le Duan Street, tel: 04-825 3949, for south-bound trains and Tran Quy Cap, tel: 04-747 0308 for north-bound.

Buses

Large express buses travel between all major towns and cities but these can be unreliable. However, an increasing number of comfortable, air-conditioned tourist buses – operated by several Vietnamese tour companies like Sinh Café *(see page 100)* – are dependable, cheap and comfortable.

will accept US dollars as payment, the exchange rate may not be as good.

Tipping

With the advent of tourism, the practice of tipping is just taking off. Tip sparingly and only where deserved. Ten percent will do.

Airport Tax

All passengers leaving on international flights have to pay a departure tax of US$12 (HCMC) and US$14 (Hanoi).

Price Differences

Because of low income levels among the Vietnamese, a state subsidy scheme for Vietnamese nationals has given rise to a two-tiered price system for some goods and services, setting one price for nationals and another for foreigners. Hotel rooms are subject to this pricing system and there is little you can do about this, although the law is set to abolish this in the near future.

GETTING AROUND

Planes

Vietnam Airlines (www.vietnamairlines.com) the national carrier, provides an increasingly professional service all over

Above: five's a crowd on this *cyclo*

Cars and Minivans

Cars and minivans are always hired with drivers. The driver will stay with the car to protect both the vehicle and your belongings, sometimes even to the extent of sleeping in the car at night. You can hire cars from local travel agents from about US$40 per day, depending on the make and model.

Taxis

In Ho Chi Minh City **Vina Taxi** (tel: 08-811 1111) and **Festival Taxi** (tel: 08-845 6456) provide an efficient metered service. In Hanoi, **Mai Linh Taxi** (tel: 04-822 2666) and **V-Taxi** (tel: 04- 821 5668) do the same.

Smaller cities generally have locally branded taxi firms. Make sure you take a 'brand' taxi. Drivers of unmarked cars masquerading as taxis have been known to mug unsuspecting passengers.

Motorcycles (Hondas)

'Honda' is the generic term used in the south for two-wheeled motorised vehicles. 'Moto' is the official term for a bike larger than 150cc, but 'honda' is still used for just about everything from 50cc mopeds to gargantuan Suzuki 1500cc motorbikes. You can rent 'hondas' from tourist cafés and bike rental shops for around US$5 per day. You are required to leave your passport behind or a cash deposit.

It is possible to ride pillion on a 'honda' with a rider, called a *xe om* (say-ohm) in effect, a 'motorcycle taxi' – for short rides around the city, or charter one for the whole day. They cost about US$0.70 for short city trips and from US$10–20 for a whole day's charter. Biking round Vietnam on your own can be an interesting form of travel. Do bear in mind that traffic congestion is growing in the large towns and you have to contend with large trucks on the highways. Roads are also notoriously bad north of Hue.

You will find sufficient spare parts and a qualified mechanic in almost every street in the country. Petrol and tyre repair shops are equally common everywhere. In more remote areas, petrol stations can be identified by a paper cone balanced on the pavement, just beside a shack.

Cyclo

Three-wheeled pedal trishaws or *cyclo* are the hallmark of Indochina. You will have to haggle (as usual) over the price. Most inner city journeys of 5–10 minutes' duration will cost less than US$1. *Cyclos* opposite the History Museum in Hanoi now offer tours of the Old Quarter for 30,000 dong per hour.

Bicycles

In cities and towns, bicycles are a good way of getting around. They can be hired from some travel agents, hotels and cafés; try **Sinh Café** (tel: 08-836 9420) in Ho Chi Minh City or go to Hang Bac Street in Hanoi. Over the last few years more cyclists have taken to touring the country on mountain bikes. You might consider bringing in your own bicycle. Most buses and trains take bicycles on board and there are repair shops in most towns. For mountain biking tours, contact **Exotissimo** (tel: 08-825 1723; www.exotissimo.com) in Ho Chi Minh City or **Buffalo Tours** (tel: 04-828 0702; www.buffalotours.com) in Hanoi.

HOURS AND HOLIDAYS

Business Hours

Most banks, public services and state-run offices work Monday to Friday, from 7.30–8.30am, closing between 4–5pm. From 11.30am– 1.30pm, most places, including banks, shut for lunch. Tourist-orientated shops work a seven-day week; they open by 9am and close between 7–9pm. Pagodas and temples open until the evening.

Public Holidays

New Year's Day	1 January
Tet	January/February*
Liberation Day	30 April
Labour Day	1 May
National Day	2 September

(*January/February; exact date is determined by the annual lunar calendar.)

ACCOMMODATION

You will find the best and widest range of accommodation in Ho Chi Minh City. To keep up with the times and to cater to increasing numbers of businessmen, many of the older city hotels have been refurbished to international standards, In Hanoi, the choice is more limited, but there are still bargains to be had. Elsewhere, standards can vary. If you're on a tight budget, try the so-called 'minihotels', ie small, often family-run hotels with fairly modern facilities. These abound in Hanoi and Ho Chi Minh City and are beginning to make an appearance in popular resort towns.

Rates are subject to 10–15 percent government tax. Published rates for a standard double room are categorised as follows:
$$$$ = US$150 and above;
$$$ = US$100–150;
$$ = US$50–100;
$ = US$50 and below.

Ho Chi Minh City

Caravelle Hotel
19–23 Lam Son Square, District 1
Tel: 08-823 4999; Fax: 08-824 3999
www.caravellehotel.com

Extensively renovated and expanded into another huge but tasteful highrise, the older 10-storey wing was a top spot with journalists during the war. Prime city location near Dong Khoi Street. $$$$

Sheraton Saigon
88 Dong Khoi Street, District 1
Tel: 08-827 2828; Fax: 08-827 2929
www.sheraton.com/saigon
Latest addition to the Saigon skyline boasting the highest bar in town and four restaurants to boot. With lavish rooms and restaurants, it has the added bonus of being located on the hippest shopping street in Ho Chi Minh City. $$$$

Renaissance Riverside Hotel
8-15 Ton Duc Thang Street, District 1
Tel: 08-822 0033; Fax: 08-823 5666
www.renaissancehotels.com/sgnbr
The Renaissance holds a commanding position on the city's waterfont with some of the best views along the Mekong River. 349 tastefully furnished rooms and full facilties. $$$

Sofitel Plaza Saigon
17 Le Duan Boulevard; District 1
Tel: 08-824 1555; Fax: 08-824 1666
www.accorhotels-asia.com
One of the first 5-star hotels in the city, the Sofitel is an elegant modern highrise with tastefully appointed rooms, Western and Asian restaurants, and a rooftop pool offering panoramic city views. $$$

Bong Sen Hotel
117-123 Dong Khoi Street
Tel: 08-829 1721; Fax: 08-829 8076
www.hotelbongsen.com
Centrally located along the city's most frequented shopping street. This large, comfortable hotel offers an alternative to some of the pricier options on Dong Khoi. $$–$$$

Continental Hotel
132 Dong Khoi Street, District 1
Tel: 08-829 9201; Fax: 08-829 0936
www.continental-saigon.com

Above: Majestic Hotel

The setting for Graham Greene's *The Quiet American*. Refurbished tastefully, the place is full of old world charm and comfort. A personal favourite of many first-time travellers to Vietnam. **$$–$$$**

Rex Hotel
141 Nguyen Hue Blvd, District 1
Tel: 08-829 2185; Fax: 08-829 6536
www.rexhotelvietnam.com
This hotel is a popular palace to faded kitsch. But it isn't the dodgy decor that appeals, it's the colourful history. The hotel housed military officers during the war and guests can still imagine generals sipping sundowners on the rooftop terrace. **$$–$$$**

Giant Dragon Hotel
173 Pham Ngu Lao Street, District 1
Tel: 08-836 1935; Fax: 08-836 4759
For a little comfort in backpackerville, try this mid-range hotel located on the main traveller thoroughfare. The hotel has 34 air-conditioned rooms and a restaurant on site. **$$**

Phu Quoc

Cassia Cottages
Ba Keo Beach (2km from airport)
Tel: 077-848 395; Fax: 077-848 396
www.cassiacottage.com
This villa offers a range of rooms, from family-sized cottages to rooms for singles or twin-share. Also available is an in-house restaurant and a new pool facing the sea. Airport pickup is provided. **$$**

Tropicana Resort
Long Beach
Tel: 077-847 127; Fax: 077-847 128
www.vngold.com/pq/tropicana
Located only 10 minutes from the town of Duong Dong, this resort features bungalows, a pool and a private beach. **$$**

Phan Thiet

Victoria Phan Thiet Resort
Km 9, Phu Hai
Tel: 062-813 000; Fax: 062-813 007
www.victoriahotels-asia.com

A luxury resort right on the beach in Phan Tiet. The Victoria features 50 cottages, most with sea views. Family cottages are also available. Full facilities, bike and car rentals, private beach, freshwater pool and jacuzzi. Be warned that the food at the hotel restaurant can be disappointing. **$$–$$$**

Coco Beach
58 Nguyen Dinh Chieu
Tel: 062-847 111; Fax: 062-847 115
www.cocobeach.net
One of the first resorts in Phan Thiet, it was opened in 1995 by an expat French and German couple. Has 34 comfortable bungalows all with sea views set among landscaped tropical gardens. The restaurant has a fantastic evening seafood grill buffet and all-day service to guests lounging on the beach. **$$**

Saigon Mui Ne Resort
55 Nguyen Dinh Chieu
Tel: 062-847 324; Fax: 062-847 307
www.saigonmuineresort.com
A series of bungalows and apartments set in a coconut palm-strewn resort with a swimming pool and jacuzzi. **$$**

Vinh Long

Tai Nguyen Hotel
60/12 Duong Mai Thang Muong 3
Tel: 070-827 235; Fax: 070-830 829
Located 5km (3 miles) outside the city centre, this hotel is the newest and by far the best in town. **$$**

Can Tho

Victoria Can Tho Hotel
Cai Khe Ward, Can Tho
Tel: 071-810 111; Fax: 071-829 259
www.victoriahotels-asia.com
Opened in October 1998, this is the most luxurious hotel in the Delta area. Located on its own promontory on the banks of the Hau River several kilometres from the centre of town, it has 88 tasteful rooms and 8 suites. With full facilities, swimming pool, and its own jetty. Restaurant offers Western and Asian food. **$$**

Saigon Can Tho Hotel
55 Phan Dinh Phung Street
Tel: 071-825 831; Fax: 071-823 288
www.saigon-cantho.com
For a stay in central Can Tho, try this comfortable, modern hotel with 46 rooms. Facilities include a business centre, conference room and fitness centre. Restaurant serves Western, Chinese and Vietnamese food. **$–$$**

Da Lat

Sofitel Da Lat Palace
12 Tran Phu
Tel: 063-825 444; Fax: 063-825 666
www.accorhotels-asia.com
The only five-star hotel in Da Lat. Luxury accommodation and excellent service amid stunning surroundings and overlooking Xuan Huong Lake. Tastefully renovated in classic French colonial style. All the usual facilities plus gourmet French restaurant and access to Da Lat Golf Course. **$$$$**

Novotel Da Lat
7 Tran Phu Street
Tel: 063-825 777; Fax: 63-825 888
www.accorhotels-asia.com
Formerly the Du Parc Hotel and extensively renovated in 1997, it is now managed by the same company that operates its neighbour, the Sofitel Da Lat Palace. Shares many of its facilities, including the restaurants and bar with the Sofitel, all of which are on the latter's premises. **$$$**

Minh Tam Villas
20A Khe Sanh
Tel: 063-822 447; Fax: 063-824 420
Located 3km from the town centre, this basic but comfortable hotel is located on the premises of a large, well kept flower garden and has 48 rooms. So popular is the garden that it is now on the usual tourist route – for a fee. **$**

Nha Trang

Ana Mandara Resort
Tran Phu Boulevard
Tel: 058-829 829; Fax: 058-829 629
www.sixsenses.com/evason-anamandara
Upscale (and very expensive) beachside resort, with 68 timbered villas set in lush tropical gardens; the pricier ones come with sea views. Features an excellent restaurant that serves Vietnamese and Western food, and a spa. **$$$$**

Nha Trang Lodge Hotel
42 Tran Phu
Tel: 058-810 500; Fax: 058-828 800
www.nt-lodge.com
This comfortable hotel on the beachfront boasts 14 floors and 132 tasteful rooms, each with an ocean view. Seafood restaurant with Asian and European dishes. Full facilities, business centre, and a swimming pool. **$$–$$$**

Bao Dai's Villas
Cau Da, Vinh Nguyen
Tel: 058-590 147; Fax: 058-590 146
www.vngold.com/nt/baodai
One of the last remaining examples of French colonial architecture, built in 1923. There are 48 rooms and 5 original villas together with 2 sea-view restaurants. Rooms are fairly basic, but you pay for the history of the place. **$–$$**

Danang

Furama Resort
68 Ho Xuan Huong
Tel: 0511-847 888; Fax: 0511-847 666
www.furamavietnam.com
Luxury resort located right on China Beach and a short drive from Danang. Elegant landscaped gardens with two swimming pools, private beach and well appointed rooms. **$$$$**

Royal Hotel
17 Quang Trung Street
Tel: 0511-823 295; Fax: 0511-827 279
e-mail: royalhotel@dng.vnn.vn
Four-storey hotel with 28 rooms located in the city centre, just 15 minutes from the airport. Small but stylish rooms and the usual facilities. **$$**

Hoi An

Victoria Hoi An Resort
1 Cua Dai Beach
Tel: 0510-927 040; Fax: 0510-927 041
www.victoriahotels-asia.com
Elegant hotel located right on a white sand beach and only 5km away from Hoi An. The Victoria has several accommodation options, with French, Vietnamese and Japanese inspired decor. Large swimming pool, restaurants, and operates a shuttle bus into Hoi An. This is by far the most expensive hotel in Hoi An, but it is worth it. **$$$**

Hoi An Riverside Resort
175 Cua Dai Road
Tel: 0510-864 800; Fax: 0510-864 900
www.hoianriverresort.com
Charming riverside location by the Do River and close to Cua Dai beach. Full range of facilities, including a swimming pool. Organises tours to attractions in the area. **$$–$$$**

Hoi An Hotel
6 Tran Hung Dao
Tel: 0510-861 373; Fax: 0510-861 636
Comfortable rooms in a colonial-style building in Hoi An town. **$$**

Hue

Century Riverside Inn
49 Le Loi Street
Tel: 054-823 390; Fax: 054-821 426
cenhotvn@dng.vnn.vn
This is Hue's most expensive hotel and it offers lovely views of the Perfume River waterfront. The full range of the usual facilities are available. **$$$**

Imperial Garden Hotel (Thanh Noi Hotel)
57 Dang Dung
Tel: 054-522 478; Fax: 054-527 211
www.viehotel.com/thanhnoihotel
Located in the heart of the old city near the citadel, this hotel features 60 rooms, a swimming pool and a garden restaurant offering European and Asian cuisine. **$$**

Lang Co Beach Resort
Lang Co Town, Phu Loc District, Thua Thien
Tel: 054-873 555; Fax: 054-873 504
langcobeachresort.huonggiangtourist.com
This beach-side resort is roughly midway between Danang (50km) and Hue (70km). Has 84 rooms and 2 restaurants serving traditional Hue dishes and seafood. **$$**

Saigon Morin Hotel
30 Le Loi
Tel: 031-823 526
www.morinhotel.com.vn
More than 100 years old, this newly renovated hotel is centrally located and offers excellent service. **$$**

Hanoi

Hotel Sofitel Metropole
15 Ngo Quyen Street
Tel: 04-826 6919; Fax: 04-826 6920
www.accorhotels-asia.com
The former Metropole dating back to 1901 is the ultimate hotel in Vietnam. Major renovations by the French Sofitel company in 1992 kept its colonial-era atmosphere intact while improving vastly on its comfort levels. Has 232 luxury rooms and two restaurants (Spices Gardens and Le Beaulieu), three bars and a swimming pool. **$$$$**

Right: Hotel Sofitel Metropole

Sheraton Hanoi Hotel
K5, Nghi Tam, 11 Xuan Dieu Road
Tel: 04-719 9000; Fax: 04-719 9001
www.sheraton.com/Hanoi
Hanoi's newest five-star, the Sheraton lies in landscaped gardens on West Lake. Facilities include a lakeside swimming pool, floodlit tennis courts, state-of-the-art conference facilities, bars and restaurants. All rooms have spacious bathrooms with separate shower and lake-views. $$$$

Hanoi Horison Hotel
40 Cat Linh Street
Tel: 04-733 0808; Fax: 04-733 0888
www.swiss-belhotel.com/hanoi.html
An imposing five-star hotel that rises somewhat pyramid-like over the skyline. The Horison has very comfortable, attractive rooms. All the usual amenities plus a great health club and swimming pool. $$$

Hilton Hanoi Opera
1 Le Thanh Tong
Tel: 04-933 0500; Fax: 04-933 0530
www.hanoi.hilton.com
Superb location and an architecturally impressive building that complements the neighbouring Opera House. Excellent facilities. The elegant facade is a popular backdrop for Vietnamese wedding shots. $$$

Melia Hanoi
44B Ly Thuong Kiet Street
Tel: 04-934 3343; Fax: 04-934 3344
www.meliahanoi.com
Located in the business and diplomatic district, this glitzy affair has 308 rooms, restaurants, bar and pool. Serves excellent Spanish food including an authentic paella. $$$

Nikko Hotel
84 Tran Nhan Tong
Tel: 04-822 3535; Fax: 04-822 3555
www.hotelnikkohanoi.com.vn
A favourite with Japanese tourists. This elegant hotel has one of the better swimming pools in town, a superb *dim sum* restaurant and the fine Japanese Benkay restaurant. $$$

De Syloia Hotel
17A Tran Hung Dao
Tel: 04-824 5346, Fax: 04-824 1083
www.desyloia.com
A small but international-quality hotel, with an excellent restaurant (Cay Cau) and gym. Situated only a few minutes away from the French Quarter and the city centre. Its 33 rooms are spacious and comfortable. $$

Moon River Retreat
Bac Cau 3, Ngoc Thuy Village
Long Bien District
Tel: 04-871 1658; Fax: 04-871 3665
New riverside retreat in a tranquil village setting, 5km (3 miles) from central Hanoi. Features traditional Asian architecture in tropical gardens, with comfortable en-suite guestrooms and fine-dining restaurant in authentic timber houses. $$

Prince Hotel
78 Hang Ga
Tel: 04-828 1332; Fax: 04-828 1636
www.princehotelhanoi.com
Centrally located in the Old Quarter and within an easy stroll from its narrow streets. Comfortable, basic en-suite rooms with air-con and IDD. $

Sa Pa

Victoria Sapa Hotel
Sapa District, Lao Cai Province
Tel: 020-871 522; Fax: 020-871 539
www.victoriahotels-asia.com
Sapa's only luxury hotel is fraying at the edges. Decent rooms and a heated swimming pool. Package deals include transfer on the luxury Victoria Express train from Hanoi. $$

Auberge Dang Trung Hotel
Sa Pa District, Lao Cai Province
Tel: 020-871 243; Fax: 020-871 666
e-mail: sapanow@yahoo.com
Charming lodge with 28 cosy rooms. The upper floor has good views of the mountain scenery if the mist clears. Ask for packages including transfers from Hanoi. $

HEALTH & EMERGENCIES

Hygiene/General Health

Always drink bottled or purified water as most Vietnamese do. Ice is best avoided outside of the major hotels. And avoid peeled fruit and food that has been exposed to flies.

Hospitals do not conform to Western standards so for serious illnesses, seek medical attention in Singapore or Bangkok. Take out a comprehensive medical insurance before you arrive, and especially if you are planning an adventure holiday.

Medical/Dental Services

If you need medical or dental attention in Ho Chi Minh City, go to the **HCM City Family Medical Practice** (tel: 08-822 7848) at Diamond Plaza, 34 Le Duan, or try the **International Medical Centre** (tel: 08-827 2366) at 1 Han Thuyen Street.

In Hanoi try the **Hanoi Family Medical Practice** (tel: 04-843 0748) at Van Phuc Diplomatic Compound, Kim Ma Road, or **Hanoi French Hospital**, 1 Phuong Mai Street (tel: 04-574 0740; www.hfh.com.vn).

Pharmacies, called *nha thuoc*, are found throughout Vietnam. Ask your hotel to recommend one.

Crime

Vietnam is generally safe and you are unlikely to have serious problems. However, minor pilfering is widespread. Be careful in markets and dark alleys. Wallets are always at risk, and you should not wear jewellery that can be easily snatched.

COMMUNICATIONS & NEWS

Post/Fax

Post offices are found in most towns and many have facilities for faxes and telexes. The main post office in Ho Chi Minh City, the **Buu Dien Ho Chi Minh**, is next to Notre Dame Cathedral (tel: 08-823 2541). In Hanoi go to the **Buu Dien Ha Noi**, 75 Dinh Tien Hoang Street (tel: 04-825 2730). Faxes can also be sent from most major hotels in HCMC and Hanoi.

Telephone

Very expensive direct calls can be placed from hotels and post offices but reverse charges are not allowed for foreigners except from the HCMC main post office.

To make an international direct dial call from Vietnam, dial the international access code: 00, followed by the country code, the area code and the local telephone number. To save on hefty international call charges, however, dial the prefix 171 or 178 before the international access code 00. These codes can also be used to call long distance within Vietnam. Alternatively, use an international calling card to call home.

Internet-connected phones can be found in many cafés and costs are significantly lower.

When calling a city in Vietnam from overseas, dial the country code 84, followed by the area code but drop the prefix zero. When making a domestic call from one province or city to another in Vietnam, dial the area code first (including the prefix zero). Note: local calls within the same province/city do not require the area code.

Note: Mobile phone numbers start with 090, 091, 095 and 098.

The area codes for the major cities mentioned in this book are as follows: Can Tho: 071; Da Lat: 063; Danang: 0511; Halong: 033; Hanoi: 04; Ho Chi Minh City: 08; Hoi An: 0510; Hue: 054; Nha Trang: 058; Phan Thiet: 062; Sa Pa: 020; Vinh Long: 070; Vung Tau: 064. Vietnam's country code is 84.

Media

At 11pm nightly, Vietnam television on Channel 9 gives the news headlines in English, and at major hotels, BBC and CNN are available. The best local English language publications are the daily broadsheet *Vietnam News*, the weekly *Vietnam Investment Review* and the monthly *Vietnam Economic Times* magazine. The Review also publishes the *Time Out* guide, a useful listings magazine.

LANGUAGE

Vietnamese is a tonal language and is almost impossible for travellers to grasp in a short space of time, although you will cause great amusement trying. Accents vary enormously from region to region. Fortunately, a Romanised script, or *quoc ngu*, is used, rendering the language readable if unpronounceable. French is spoken by older people, and English is very popular as a second language, particularly among younger people.

USEFUL ADDRESSES

Travel Agents

Ho Chi Minh City

Sinh Café
246-248 De Tham, District 1
Tel: 08-836 7338; Fax: 08-836 9322
www.sinhcafevn.com
Reliable outfit that caters mainly to the backpacker crowd.

Exotissimo
37 Ton Duc Thang, District 1
Tel: 08-825 1723; Fax: 08-829 5800
www.exotissimo.com
A leading tour operator in the Mekong region – handling groups, incentives, adventure, nature and special-interest travel.

Ann Tours
58 Ton That Tung Street, District 1
Tel: 08-833 4356
www.anntours.com
A professional private outfit offering everything from ticket booking to organised tours. Friendly service and knowlegeable guides.

Hanoi

Buffalo Tours
11 Hang Muoi
Tel: 04-828 0702; Fax: 04-826 9370
www.buffalotours.com
Reputable agent offering moderately-priced tours of Vietnam. Also organises a range of soft adventure tours.

Exotissimo
26 Tran Nhat Duat Street
Tel: 04-828 2150; Fax: 04-828 2146
www.exotissimo.com
Offers quality tailor-made and scheduled tours, travel services and adventure trips all over Vietnam. Prices are quite high but you get excellent service.

Handspan Adventure Travel
80 Ma May
Tel: 04-933 2375; Fax: 04-933 2378
www.handspan.com
Applies an 'eco-ethos' concept to tourism in Vietnam with tailor-made and value-formoney tours involving adventure kayaking, mountain biking, 4WD tours, trekking as well as more sedate journeys.

Tourism Office

Vietnam's tourism industry lags behind that of other Asian countries. Even in the capital, you won't find official tourist information kiosks giving out impartial free information. The official representative and responsibility for Vietnam's tourism – domestically and overseas – comes under the governmental Vietnam **National Administration of Tourism** (VNAT; www.vietnamtourism. com), more involved in new hotels and infrastructure investments than providing tourist services. State-run 'tourist offices' under the VNAT (or local provincial organisations) are merely tour agents out to make money and are not geared to Western requirements. For tours, car hire, information, go to private-run tour agencies, but use established, reliable outfits.

Maps are obtainable from bookstores on Trang Tien Street, or hotel receptions. Hanoi tourist information, maps and listings are found in English-language magazines: *Vietnam Discovery*, *Vietnam Pathfinder*, *The Guide* (*Vietnam Economic Times* supplement), *Time Out* (*Vietnam Investment Review* supplement) and *Vietnam Heritage* (Vietnam Airlines in-flight magazine). Call 1080 for a state-run telephone information service – with English-speaking staff.

ACKNOWLEDGEMENTS

Cover	**Jim Holmes**
Backcover	**Jim Holmes**
Photography	**Jim Holmes and**
Pages 31, 32	**Courtesy of Rainbow Divers**
34	**Hbfrbar/HBL**
21, 28, 29T, 30, 47, 55B, 56, 57, 58B,	
59, 63, 65, 67, 68T, 99	**David Henley/CPA**
20, 97	**David Henley/APA**
8/9	**Catherine Karnow**
94	**Leonardo Media**
87	**Joe Lynch/Photobank**
33	**S. Nardvlli/HBL**
51	**Tim Page**
Cartography	**Berndtson & Berndtson**
Cover Design	**Carlotta Junger**
Production	**Tanvir Virdee/Caroline Low**

INDEX